THE COMPLETE IDIOT'S GUIDE® TO

Quitting Smoking

by Lowell Kleinman, M.D., and Deborah Messina-Kleinman, M.P.H.

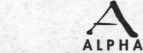

ALPHA

A member of Penguin Group (USA) Inc.

AMI

AMERICAN
MEDIA, INC.

The Complete Idiot's Guide® to Quitting Smoking

Table of Contents

Introduction

If you're like most smokers, you've tried to quit several times before. But for one reason or another, you went back to smoking. That's because quitting smoking is very challenging. It requires you to change lifelong behaviors, and that's never an easy thing to do.

Wanting to quit is half the battle. *Knowing how* to quit is the other half. That's where this book comes in. While we can't make you want to quit, we can show you the best ways to do it. If you read this book, we guarantee that you will be a better quitter. You may not quit for good on your first try—quitting involves learning a new set of skills and takes practice—lots of practice—but you'll get it eventually.

Some Extras Just for You

In addition to the text, which is chock-full of information that will help you want to quit and to stay quit once and for all, every chapter offers you the following sidebars:

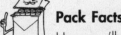

Pack Facts

Here you'll learn all kinds of interesting tidbits about tobacco, cigarettes, smokers, quitting, and more.

Quit Tips

We offer you these tips, based on our years of experience as quit-smoking coaches, to help you quit smoking for good.

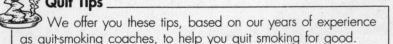

Smoking Signals

These sidebars define unfamiliar words and terms used in the book.

Smoke Alarm _____

Designed to make the quitting process easier, these side-bars warn you about the dangers of smoking, steer you clear of quitting pitfalls, and more.

Buttkicker _____

We've designed these exercises to highlight quit-smoking points and help you succeed at staying smoke-free.

Trademarks

All terms mentioned in this book that are known to be or are suspected of being trademarks or service marks have been appropriately capitalized. Alpha Books and Penguin Group (USA) Inc. cannot attest to the accuracy of this information. Use of a term in this book should not be regarded as affecting the validity of any trademark or service mark.

Chapter 1

So, You're Thinking About Quitting Smoking

In This Chapter

◆ Learn why quitting smoking is so tough

◆ Identify the three components of your tobacco addiction

◆ Know how tobacco affects your body

◆ Know the benefits of quitting smoking at any age

◆ Specify your personal reasons to quit

◆ Determine if you are really ready to quit

If you're like most people who smoke, you enjoy smoking. Many non-smokers around you just don't seem to grasp this simple fact. Whether it's your spouse, your doctor, or a coworker, those well-meaning friends and family members simply don't get it. You *like* to smoke!

And let's face it, no one has to tell you that smoking isn't good for you. Nor does anybody have to tell you that you should quit. In fact, the more that people tell you that you should quit, the less you want to. The truth of the matter is that no one can make you quit. However, chances are that you've tried to quit before—probably more than once. But for one reason or another, you picked up "just one" ciga-rette and before you knew it, you found yourself right back where you started. This cycle can be so frustrating that many smokers throw their hands in the air and stop trying to quit, at least for a while.

Now you're thinking about quitting (again), and this time for good. Bravo for you! And the really good news is that this time things will be different. This time you have a partner. Try to imagine this book and its authors as being your very own personal coaches, your very own supportive partners who understand exactly what you are going through, and who have helped thousands of people, just like you, quit smoking. We are here to walk you through the process of quitting, one step at a time. Let's get started.

This Book's for You

This book offers you a lot of information, tips, and warnings, and it's easy to get overwhelmed. To make it easier for many of the important points to stick, we repeat them from time to time. We've found that repeating important concepts helps people trying to change ingrained habits like smoking tobacco. Bear with us as we offer this technique.

It may be hard to imagine yourself as a nonsmoker right now, but by the time you complete this book, you will feel great about yourself and your new smoke-free lifestyle. Millions of people have quit smoking successfully, and you can too. So let's get started.

Why Is It So Hard to Quit Smoking?

For the vast majority of smokers, quitting is a struggle—a huge battle. Although 90 percent of people who smoke say they would like to quit (and most have tried), very few people actually make it the first time. In fact, most people have to quit about five times before they actually get it right.

Like many other things in life, quitting smoking takes a lot of practice. Remember when you were first learning to ride a bicycle? Sure, you fell off a few times, probably even got banged up a little, but eventually you were able to ride with confidence. Well, quitting smoking is just like learning to ride a bicycle. You may fall off a few times, but if you keep on practicing, you will get it right.

> **Quit Tips**
> Begin to take note of when you light up. By becoming aware of what's happening when you smoke, you will be preparing yourself for a successful quit attempt. For example, are there times you smoke because of stress? How about when you are bored or lonely?

Fighting Three Battles

Why is it so hard to quit smoking? As you'll see, everyone who tries to quit smoking is actually fighting three battles at once. Let's take a closer look at the three aspects of the tobacco addiction that each smoker must learn to conquer.

Habit

When you first began smoking, you probably had no more than a few cigarettes each day. Over time, you began to associate each cigarette with certain activities. For example, you may have had a cigarette every time you had a cup of coffee, finished dinner, or sipped a cocktail. Eventually, it seemed as if something was missing if you didn't have a cigarette at these times. All of these situations are examples of how you've taught your brain to make a connection between smoking a cigarette and doing some sort of specific activity. You formed a *habit*.

> **Smoking Signals**
> A **habit** is a behavioral response caused by frequent repetition of the same act. If you repeatedly smoke while you perform certain activities (drinking coffee, driving your car), you have a well-ingrained habit.

Physical Addiction

Don't ever underestimate the power of nicotine. It is one of the most addictive drugs on the face of the earth. Naturally found in tobacco plants, nicotine can both stimulate and relax you. In small doses, like when you take a small puff, nicotine stimulates you. In larger doses, like when you inhale the smoke deeply, it relaxes you.

Nicotine is the ingredient in your cigarettes that keeps you coming back for more. When you inhale cigarette smoke, nicotine enters your bloodstream and "hits" your brain in seven seconds. Over time, your body becomes used to having a certain amount of nicotine in your blood. When your body senses that it has less nicotine than it's used to, you begin to crave cigarettes and experience other uncomfortable symptoms. Your body makes it physically uncomfortable for you not to smoke by creating *nicotine withdrawal symptoms*.

> **Smoking Signals** _____
>
> **Nicotine withdrawal symptoms** are those emotional and physical symptoms that occur when you stop smoking. They include irritability, difficulty concentrating, anxiety, and strong cravings for a cigarette.

If you've been a smoker for awhile, chances are good that you've experienced nicotine withdrawal at some time in your life. For example, try to recall a time when you had to go longer than usual without a cigarette. Perhaps you were on an airplane or trapped in a business meeting. Whatever the reason, you probably started to crave a cigarette as the nicotine levels in your blood began to drop. As the levels fell even lower, you probably had difficulty concentrating, and you may even have become irritable. People around you may have said you seemed grouchy, scatter-brained, or edgy. These are some of the symptoms of nicotine withdrawal, and they mean that you are physically addicted to cigarettes.

Psychological Dependence

Do you ever find yourself lighting up when you are feeling angry, frustrated, lonely, or bored? If you do, you may use smoking as a way to cope with unpleasant feelings or emotions. How did you learn to do this?

Remember when we said that nicotine could both stimulate and relax you? Well, that's how people become psychologically addicted to nicotine. For example, if you are bored while waiting in line, you may want to smoke for the stimulant effect. Similarly, if you're feeling angry or frustrated because you're stuck in traffic, you may find yourself smoking as a way of calming down. Basically, you've learned how to use nicotine as an artificial mood moderator.

Practice Makes Perfect

In this book, you will learn all of the skills you need to fight the three battles surrounding tobacco addiction: habit, physical addiction, and psychological dependence. Be patient with yourself, practice these techniques, and you, too, will be a successful quitter.

The Truth About the Health Effects of Tobacco

Do people who care about you keep asking you to quit smoking because it's bad for your health? Although it can be annoying, let's face it, they're right. (On the other hand, being hounded all the time can't be too good for you, either.) The fact is, tobacco is the number one cause of preventable death and disease in the United States and Canada and is a leading cause of illness and death in many other countries. Worldwide, it is directly responsible for three million deaths each year. It is a leading cause of heart disease, stroke, many cancers, *emphysema*, and *chronic bronchitis*. (Are we sounding like your Aunt Harriet yet?)

> **Smoking Signals**
>
> **Emphysema** involves damage to tiny air sacs in your lungs by cigarette smoke, which makes it difficult for oxygen to go from the lungs into the bloodstream. **Chronic bronchitis** involves an irritation and inflammation of the airways in your lungs from exposure to cigarette smoke. Together, emphysema and chronic bronchitis are known as C.O.P.D. (Chronic Obstructive Pulmonary Disease).

The Junk in Your Cigarettes

Tobacco smoke contains over 4,000 chemicals, at least 63 of which have been proven to cause cancer in humans (as if one weren't enough). In addition to lung cancer, tobacco use causes cancer of the lip, tongue, throat, esophagus, bladder, cervix, and kidney—just about every important organ in your body. Here are just a few of the chemicals found in your cigarettes:

◆ Nicotine (also used as an insecticide to kill bugs)

◆ Carbon monoxide (the same colorless, odorless gas that comes out of the tailpipe of your car)

◆ Tar (very similar in color and consistency to the tar used to pave the highway)

◆ Hydrogen cyanide (also known as gas chamber poison)

◆ Arsenic (the infamous poison used to kill the victim in many murder mysteries)

◆ Methane (a byproduct of eating too many beans at dinner)

Let's take a look at just how several of these chemicals can cause so much damage to your body.

◆ **Nicotine.** This chemical is at least as addictive as alcohol, heroin, and cocaine. Within seven seconds after inhaling cigarette smoke, nicotine reaches your brain (that's faster than an intravenous drug). As if they were under attack by a pair of vice grips, your blood vessels are squeezed together causing your blood pressure to rise. This increases your risk for strokes and heart attacks.

- **Carbon monoxide.** As you inhale cigarette smoke, your lungs are filled with air that contains high levels of carbon monoxide. Your red blood cells get confused. Instead of picking up the oxygen, they go for the carbon monoxide. (Don't ask us why they are so easily fooled!) The end result is that less oxygen reaches your organs, and your risk for having a heart attack or stroke increases.

- **Tar.** While tar is good for our highways, it's not good for your lungs. Your lungs have tiny little hairlike structures in them called cilia. Cilia look like bristles on a brush, and they are responsible for sweeping your lungs clean. All day long, the cilia in healthy lungs sweep out the germs and particles of dust we breathe in. Unfortunately, tar inhaled through cigarette smoke sticks to your cilia, making them unable to perform their cleaning action. Your airways begin to swell and get clogged up with mucus. This is why people who smoke get more colds and develop a "smoker's cough." Many go on to develop chronic bronchitis (inflammation of the airways) and emphysema (permanent rupturing of the tiny air sacs). As if this isn't enough, it's the tar that contains many of the *carcinogens*, or cancer-causing agents, found in cigarettes.

Sharing Your Smoke with Others

Smokers aren't the only ones who are inhaling the cigarette smoke. The people around them also inhale the smoke and suffer from the ill effects of cigarettes. *Secondhand smoke* is responsible for many illnesses, including asthma, chronic bronchitis, heart disease, and cancer. The sad truth is that 50,000 people in the United States die every year because of secondhand smoke. This is why many people who smoke choose to smoke outdoors or in another room to protect the people they care about.

Smoking Signals

Secondhand smoke includes both the smoke from the burning end of a cigarette and the smoke exhaled by the smoker.

Some people who smoke question whether or not secondhand smoke is dangerous. Some believe that it is just propaganda put forth by groups interested in seeing smokers stop using cigarettes in public. However, the facts are in. Secondhand smoke is, without a doubt, a bad player and does cause a lot of harm.

Quitting Smoking Is Good for You at Any Age

Okay, enough of that. Now it's time for some good news that will help you focus on quitting. Quitting smoking now will greatly improve your health and life no matter how long you've been smoking. That's right, no matter how long you've been smoking. Whether you have smoked for 5 years or 50, your body is an amazing machine that can heal much of the damage caused by years of tobacco use. In fact, your body starts to recover within 20 minutes of your last cigarette!

The Health Benefits of Quitting

Time After Your Last Cigarette	Benefit to Your Body
20 minutes	Blood pressure and pulse rate decrease to normal
8 hours	Carbon monoxide levels in blood drop and oxygen levels increase
24 hours	Chance of heart attack decreases
48 hours	Food tastes and smells better
	Nerve endings begin to regrow
72 hours	Bronchial tubes relax and breathing becomes easier

Time After Your Last Cigarette	Benefit to Your Body
2 weeks to 3 months	Coughing, congestion, tiredness, and shortness of breath decrease
	Overall energy increases
	Walking becomes easier
1 to 9 months	Cilia regrow in the lungs
	Shortness of breath decreases
1 year	Risk of heart disease is half that of a smoker
5 years	Chance of lung cancer decreased by almost a half
10 to 15 years	Pre-cancerous cells are replaced
	Risk of dying is similar to that of someone who has never smoked

Wow! What great reasons to stop smoking. But wait, there's more ...

Other Benefits of Quitting

The benefits of quitting smoking include more than better health. You'll save lots of money, regain control over your life, and set a better example for children in your family and in your community, to name just a few. If you ask successful ex-smokers about the benefits of quitting, many will include feeling a sense of pride and accomplishment, being more productive at work, having better relationships with family members, improved appetite, more energy, enhanced sense of taste and smell, cleaner clothing, whiter teeth, fresher breath, improved appearance, and better sex. What more could you ask for?

The amount of money spent on tobacco products each year is staggering. (No wonder the tobacco companies work so hard to keep their customers addicted.) Now, let's look at this another way. How much money would you save if you quit now? What would you do with it?

> **Buttkicker** _____
> ### The Co$t of $moking and Dipping
> Just how much do you spend each year on tobacco? Let's take a look:
>
> ___ packs/tins per day × 7 = ___ (packs/tins per week)
>
> ___ packs/tins per week × $___ (cost per pack/tin) =
> $___ (cost per week)
>
> $___ (cost per week) × 52 = $___ (cost per year)

Your Reasons to Quit

Now it's time to stop and think. What are _your_ reasons to quit? (Not your friends' reasons and not your relatives' reasons—your reasons.) Think about all of the possible benefits of quitting smoking _for you_, both short-term and long-term. We recommend that you make a very detailed, specific list right now. Try to think not only about _your_ health, but also the health of those around you. Consider things such as the cost of cigarettes, feelings about yourself, your ability to take control over your life, and the example you may be setting for others. Also, think about how you would like to see yourself five or ten years from now.

> **Buttkicker** _____
> List at least two other specific ways you could use this amount of money (the amount you spend each year):
>
> **1.** _____
> **2.** _____
>
> If you can't think of any, you could always send it to the authors. We'll spend it for you.

> **Buttkicker**
>
> **My Top Five Reasons to Quit**
>
> After you've made a thorough, detailed list of all of the potential benefits you could gain from quitting smoking, choose your five most important reasons and write them here.
>
> 1._____
> 2._____
> 3._____
> 4._____
> 5._____

It's very important to be clear about what you hope to gain from quitting smoking. This will help to keep you focused and on track when the going gets tough. Now that you know why you want to quit, let's make sure that now is the right time for you to do so.

Are You Really Ready to Quit Smoking?

Let's face it, life is full of challenges. But it is through these challenges that we grow as individuals. This may sound a little "fortune-cookie-ish," but quitting smoking is one of the biggest challenges you will ever undertake. Rest assured that once you conquer this one, you'll know that you can do just about anything else you set your mind to. So, now it's time for you to think about whether or not you are ready for this challenge. One way to figure out if you are ready to quit is to see what stage of quitting you are in. Let's look at the six stages of quitting smoking.

Two very smart researchers with entirely too much free time on their hands have figured out that most people who smoke go through six psychological stages before they quit. They called them "The Stages of Change," and most people will cycle through these six stages several times before quitting successfully. Let's review these stages and see which one you are in at this time.

Stage 1: Pre-Contemplation

In this stage, the person has no desire to quit. There is no thought ever given to the idea of quitting smoking. He or she likes smoking, and that's that. Only 10 percent of smokers are in this stage at any given time. (People in this stage probably won't be reading this book.)

Stage 2: Contemplation

In this stage, the individual is just thinking about quitting smoking. He or she is not ready to do anything about it but rather is just starting to think about the effects of smoking or what it might be like to quit. Most smokers make it at least to this stage, although some get "stuck" here. (We call them "chronic contemplators.")

Stage 3: Preparation

Here, the person is not only thinking about quitting, but he or she is actually doing something about it. For example, he or she may switch brands, cut down on the number of cigarettes smoked each day, or buy a good book on quitting smoking. This person is building up the desire to quit and the commitment to stick with it.

Stage 4: Action

In this stage, the individual is no longer smoking. He or she is actually in the midst of trying to quit. The smoker is usually feeling very motivated about not smoking and is trying to cope with the physical and psychological aspects of quitting. It is a difficult, ongoing battle for many people who quit and requires the use of special new skills.

Stage 5: Maintenance

Here we have a person who has quit for a period of time, usually six months or so. Now he or she is working on staying quit. Here we see that although the individual is becoming more comfortable with not smoking, there are still some very challenging situations that arise. The ex-smoker's resolve will be periodically put to the test. Don't worry, we will prepare you for this stage.

Stage 6: Relapse

In this stage, the individual has gone back to smoking after trying to stay quit for a while. It's extremely important to recognize that this is a normal, natural stage in the quitting process! The tendency is to say something like, "I've failed. This is too hard, and I can't do it." Nothing could be further from the truth. Not only is relapse a normal part of quitting, it's one of the best ways to learn why you really smoke and what you must do differently next time to succeed. It is not uncommon to cycle through this stage several times before finally quitting for good. So, if this has happened to you, don't beat up on yourself. Remember, it took you several tries before you were able to ride that bicycle.

Am I Ready for Action?

So what stage are you in? Are you someone who has relapsed several times? Are you primed and ready for action? One important point needs to be made: if you are past Stage 1, it's important to recognize the progress you've made and that you are well on your way to quitting smoking for good. Just thinking about taking on the challenge of quitting is an incredible feat. Hooray for you!

The fact is that no one can make you quit. Only you can decide when it's time to leave the pack behind. Although the sooner you quit, the better it will be for you and those around you, it's important to decide whether or not now is the right time. *Note that there will never be a perfect time to quit.* Answer these questions honestly to help you decide if now is the right time for you:

- Do you have at least one specific, personal reason to quit smoking?

- Are your top five reasons to quit very important to you?

- Are you willing to experience some temporary discomfort in order to achieve your goal?

- Can you name at least one person who will be supportive of your efforts to quit?

- Would you be willing to possibly gain some weight (temporarily) in order to quit smoking for good?

If you answered "yes" to at least two of the five questions, you should continue to move forward with your decision to quit smoking. The more "yes" responses you have, the better.

If you answered "no" to four or more of the five questions, right now may not be the best time for you to try to quit smoking. Give yourself a little time, and then answer the questions again in a month or so. You may even want to talk with some people who have quit smoking to find out why they did it, what they've gained, and whether or not they believe it was worth the effort.

The Least You Need to Know

- Be patient with yourself because smoking is a complex behavior that involves habit, psychological dependence, and physical addiction.

- Remember that smoking is a leading cause of death and disease.

- Know that quitting smoking at any age will give you enormous health benefits.

- Millions of people have quit successfully, and you can, too!

- Know your own specific, personal reasons for quitting.

- Decide if now is the right time for you to quit smoking.

Chapter 2

Patch Things Up

In This Chapter

◆ Learn about quit-smoking medications, including the nicotine patch

◆ Understand the differences amongst nicotine patches

◆ Learn about combination strategies

In this chapter, we focus on one of the most commonly used quit-smoking medications, the nicotine patch. As is the case with all of the quit-smoking medications, nicotine patches have been proven to greatly increase your chances of quitting. (Actually, they just about double your chances.) You can even combine the patch with other quit-smoking methods to really maximize your chances of success.

Know the Limits

Before we get started discussing quit-smoking medications, it's important to recognize that each of these medications has its limitations. While each medication can definitely improve your odds of successfully quitting, none of them can make you want to quit. Only you can do that.

For example, the nicotine patch can prevent many of the symptoms of nicotine withdrawal, and this can be a real boost to your quit-smoking efforts. But the patch—or any other medication—can't motivate you or change your mind about quitting, which means that quitting will still take a lot of motivation and self-determination. It's hard work for most people, and there are no magic bullets. (We wish there were!)

It's also important to know that many of the quit-smoking medications focus on easing the discomfort of nicotine withdrawal. That's definitely a good thing, because nicotine withdrawal is public enemy number one for someone trying to quit smoking. In fact, nicotine withdrawal is responsible for most "failed" quit attempts. But don't worry. Knowing about nicotine addiction will make you better prepared to face this enemy.

Hindsight Is "20/20"

If you have tried to quit before, you may have used one of these medications already. The fact that you are trying to quit again doesn't mean that the medication failed you or that you should try something else. Maybe you weren't fully ready to quit, or maybe you used the medication incorrectly. (Many people don't chew nicotine gum correctly, for instance.) Before discarding a previously tried method, it's important to know why it didn't work. If you did, that would be like junking a car that didn't start up one morning without checking to see why.

Before you completely write off a previously tried medication, decide whether it helped you in any way. If it did, you may want to incorporate it into your next quit attempt. Above all, remember that relapsing is a normal and expected part of the quitting cycle. More likely than not, the medication didn't fail you. You just experienced a normal and expected part of the quit-smoking cycle, the relapse.

Nicotine Replacement Therapies

Some of the most powerful quit-smoking methods currently available are called the nicotine replacement therapies (NRT). Currently available therapies include nicotine patches, gums, nasal sprays, and inhalers. Each of these products focuses on replacing the nicotine you get from your cigarettes with nicotine from the product. Basically, they all work the same way. By very gradually reducing your nicotine exposure (over several months), you are able to slowly taper off the number of cigarettes you smoke without experiencing any major symptoms of withdrawal.

To better understand how these products work, we need to review nicotine addiction. By now, your body has gotten very used to seeing nicotine on a frequent basis (for example, every time you smoke). Nicotine has been like a great "friend" who is always there for you. This friend helps you during times of stress by helping to control your moods. It's always there when you are bored and helps you concentrate. How nice!

Pack Facts

For the average tobacco user, NRT maintains a nicotine level that is lower than when smoking, but high enough to eliminate, or at least take the bite out of, withdrawal symptoms. The beauty of these products is that they enable you to quit more comfortably (without the "crazies") while eliminating the other 4,000 chemicals found in tobacco products.

When you quit smoking, your body suddenly has to go without nicotine. All of a sudden, you have to function without your friend, maybe for the first time in many years. In response to your friend's absence, your body freaks out and you get nervous, anxious, irritable, or depressed (a normal reaction to losing one so dear). This is the essence of nicotine withdrawal.

Let's look at this scenario again, but this time through the eyes of a scientist. For many years, your brain has been frequently exposed to high levels of nicotine, which affected your brain by creating a large number of nicotine *receptors*. When these receptors are physically in touch with nicotine, cells in the brain release "good feeling" chemicals, which cause you to feel good, help control your mood, suppress your appetite, and relax you. When you quit smoking, these receptors aren't exposed to the regular amount of nicotine, and thus those "good feeling" chemicals aren't released. Instead of feeling up, you feel irritable and depressed. That's the withdrawal part.

> **Smoking Signals**
>
> A **receptor** is a structure on the surface of brain cells to which chemicals like nicotine attach. Once attached to receptors, nicotine triggers a chemical reaction that causes you to experience certain feelings, such as calmness.

With NRT, however, the nicotine receptors in the brain receive just enough nicotine to prevent withdrawal symptoms from occurring—and without the added tar and other cancer-causing chemicals. Over time, the nicotine receptors in your brain get used to receiving less and less nicotine as you gradually decrease the dose of the nicotine replacement product you are using. After several months, your brain no longer needs the nicotine to feel good, and you have quit. Now, isn't that simple?

> **Quit Tips**
>
> See your doctor for advice before using NRT. People with stomach ulcers, thyroid disease, heart problems, high blood pressure, diabetes, kidney or liver disease, or asthma should check with their doctor before using one of these products.

Nicotine Patches

Nicotine patches were initially available by prescription only. Most patches may now be purchased over-the-counter. Some of the nicotine patch brands that you may recognize include Nicoderm CQ, Nicotrol, and Habitrol. There are also generic brands out on the market. All patches are worn on the body like a bandage, and release a steady amount of nicotine that your skin absorbs and sends into the bloodstream and through the blood to the brain.

The patches have an adhesive backing that allows them to stick to your body. They must be placed on a nonhairy area of your body because hair would interfere with the absorption of the nicotine. (You are out of luck if you live with a gorilla that smokes.) The patches are changed every day, and a new one is applied.

The patches come in different strengths. Nicoderm CQ and Habitrol come as 21 mg, 14 mg, and 7 mg doses. Nicotrol comes in a 15 mg dose. Which level you should start with depends upon your level of smoking. The patches are generally worn for 8 to 12 weeks.

The following table can help you decide where to start.

Number of Cigarettes Smoked/Day	Nicoderm CQ	Nicotrol	Habitrol
0 to 10	7 mg or 14 mg	15 mg	7 mg or 14 mg
10 to 20	14 mg or 21 mg	15 mg	14 mg or 21 mg
>20	21 mg	15 mg	21 mg

In our opinion, there aren't any major differences between the patches. Perhaps the biggest difference is that Nicotrol and Nicoderm CQ are available over-the-counter and Habitrol requires a prescription. Otherwise, they all work the same way.

Most people tolerate nicotine patches without any side effects. However, some people do complain of headaches, nausea, upset stomach, dizziness, and irritation at the placement site. Some of these symptoms are just part of nicotine withdrawal, but they can also occur if your patch dose is too high.

Some people also complain of having nightmares after starting the patch. This is probably because most people who smoke don't wake up in the middle of the night for a cigarette. (Although we know of some very addicted smokers who do.) Since your body is not used to getting nicotine while you are asleep, the patches can cause nightmares. Any of the patches can be removed just before bedtime if nightmares are a problem. The downside is that you may wake up with a big fat craving first thing in the morning.

When you put on a patch, you may experience some burning or itching at the site, but these symptoms are usually gone in one to two hours. Upon removal, the area where the patch was may remain red for a day or two. You probably shouldn't use a patch if you have an allergy to adhesive tape. Discuss the matter with your doctor.

Nicotine patches aren't inexpensive. A two-week supply costs about $50, no matter what dose you use. Think of it this way: If you currently smoke a pack a day, you'll spend about the same for the patch as you do for cigarettes every week. And remember, you'll only use the patch for a few months, whereas the cost of smoking can last (and take) a lifetime.

Nicotine can be toxic if swallowed in large amounts so be careful to keep these products out of the reach of children and pets. Even after you've used a patch for 24 hours, it still contains enough nicotine to make a young person or animal very sick if he or she ingests it.

One of the most important things to know about the nicotine patch is that it is never to be worn while you are smoking. Using the patch while you smoke can result in dangerously high levels of nicotine in your body. Not only can this make you feel very ill, it can possibly cause you to have a heart attack.

Pack Facts _____

Nicotine patches are well tolerated by most people. The most commonly reported side effect is some skin irritation at the placement site. You can usually place an over-the-counter steroid cream at the area of irritation for treatment if this occurs.

I'll Try the Combo Platter

Generally speaking, nicotine patches shouldn't be combined with other forms of nicotine replacement therapy. For example, you shouldn't regularly use the nicotine nasal spray while wearing a patch. This could potentially cause you to get sick from being exposed to too much nicotine.

You may have noticed that we said, "generally speaking, nicotine patches shouldn't be combined with other forms of nicotine replacement therapy." There are some individuals who are so heavily addicted to nicotine (three-to-four-packs-a-day smokers) that they can benefit from using more than one form of nicotine replacement therapy. However, this should only be done under a doctor's guidance.

Quit Tips

As long as you check with your doctor first, you might be able to combine two or more NRTs to help you quit, especially if you're extremely addicted to nicotine after smoking three to four packs a day.

Pros of the Nicotine Patch

- Easy to use

- Private—no one has to know you are using one

- Some are available over-the-counter

- Tames nicotine withdrawal symptoms so that you are able to focus your energy on quitting

- Doubles your chances of successfully quitting

- Can be combined with other quit-smoking methods

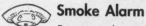 **Smoke Alarm** _____

> Because the patches contain nicotine, they may interfere with certain asthma and depression medications. There may be some problems if you have high blood pressure or heart problems, so even though they are available over-the-counter, talk with your doctor first. Also, talk to your doctor if you are breastfeeding or pregnant and want to use a nicotine patch.

Cons of the Nicotine Patch

◆ Somewhat costly

◆ May cause side effects

◆ Requires being exposed to a medication

◆ May cause nightmares

In the end, however, the most important advice we can give you is to visit your doctor and talk to him or her. Your doctor knows you, the strength of your nicotine addiction, and the state of your health best— or at least better than we do! He or she is in the best position to evaluate your need for, and to monitor if necessary, the use of the patch.

The Least You Need to Know

◆ Quit-smoking medications significantly lessen the symptoms of nicotine withdrawal.

◆ Quit-smoking medications double your chances of quitting.

◆ Most people who have quit smoking relapse within the first 72 hours.

◆ Nicotine patches cost about the same amount of money as a pack-a-day habit.

◆ Nicotine patches can be combined with other quit-smoking methods.

Less Traditional Tools of the Trade

In This Chapter

- ◆ Learn about hypnosis and acupuncture
- ◆ Learn about herbs, aromatherapy, imagery, and meditation
- ◆ Realize that there is no one best way to quit
- ◆ Know that methods from this chapter can be combined with some of the methods from other chapters

This chapter reviews several less traditional quit-smoking methods, such as acupuncture, hypnosis, and aromatherapy. Just because these methods are less traditional, however, doesn't mean they are less useful or that they won't work for you.

The less traditional methods don't always have formal studies conducted by researchers that determine their effectiveness. (Harvard has yet to study the effect of aromatherapy on smoking cessation, for instance.) Despite this, we encourage you to use your logic and judge whether or not a less traditional method makes sense to you. And remember, it's always wise to combine more than one method.

The fact that many of these methods haven't been studied as extensively as the nicotine replacement therapies has a lot to do with money. Pharmaceutical companies stand to make a lot of money by selling patches, gums, and pills, which means that they're willing to pour millions of dollars into a formal, scientific study that can pass the scrutiny of the U.S. Food and Drug Administration (FDA). Hypnotists and acupuncturists don't usually have that kind of money, so they can't necessarily promote and study their methods like the big boys do.

We suggest that you read this chapter with an open mind. Think about what has worked for you in the past and what hasn't. Consider all of your options before coming to a final decision about how you are going to quit.

Hypnosis

Hypnosis is one of the methods most frequently used by individuals wanting to quit smoking. Some people who have quit swear by this method, while many others feel as though they wasted their time and money.

The goal of the hypnotist is to create a light trance so that the quit-smoking suggestions he or she offers can replace the desire and urge to smoke. Alternative behaviors are suggested to replace the desire for smoking. The cost can vary but typically runs about $60 per hour.

There aren't a lot of good studies evaluating the effectiveness of hypnosis on quitting smoking. One study showed that 23 percent of people who were hypnotized weren't smoking 6 months later. But according to the Agency for Health Care Policy and Research, the rates drop off dramatically by about one year.

Given these facts, many people who use hypnosis to quit like to combine it with some other method, like a good cessation program or a medication. This way, the behavioral issues and nicotine withdrawal can also be addressed.

Finding a good hypnotist may be a challenge because there aren't any good accrediting agencies for these professionals. If you choose this method, you will probably need to rely on friends and your personal doctors for a good recommendation. Hypnotists are typically not physicians because the subject is not taught in most medical schools.

The number of sessions needed varies depending upon the hypnotist and you. Some people are smoke-free after one session, while others require up to four sessions. Sessions may be conducted on an individual basis or in a group setting. One-on-one sessions typically last about an hour, whereas group sessions typically last several hours. Most hypnotists feel the individual approach has a better success rate than the group setting.

Quit Tips

Some of the less traditional methods reviewed in this chapter lack hard and fast evidence of their efficacy. Use your best judgment, and ask your doctor or a trusted health professional before you decide if a particular method is right for you.

The Pros of Hypnosis

- Doesn't involve medications
- May require only one visit
- Good for people who feel their problem is a lack of willpower (although this is usually an oversimplification)

The Cons of Hypnosis

- Can get expensive
- Doesn't address nicotine addiction
- Not proven to work in the long run
- Doesn't teach you how to stay quit or how to handle difficult situations

Our advice: Although evidence is lacking for long-term success, it can be a good choice to use as a jump start, as long as it's combined with a more traditional method.

Acupuncture

Acupuncture is an old Chinese medical tradition that stimulates the body to heal itself naturally. It's based on a theory that there are channels of energy that move in regular patterns throughout the body. These energy channels, also called meridians, bring nourishing chemicals to the tissues of your body. Anything that blocks these channels from working can affect the health of the individual. Acupuncture needles are placed into acupuncture points to undo any blockages, thus restoring the body to its natural healthy balance.

Modern medicine views acupuncture as a method that stimulates the nervous system to release natural chemicals into your circulation. These chemicals decrease pain and also affect the way your organs work. The end result is a stimulation of the body's natural healing ability.

Acupuncture is used to deal with these three areas:

- Preventing diseases
- Treating diseases
- Promoting health and well-being

Many people who smoke report that acupuncture reduced the withdrawal symptoms when they stopped smoking. One particular method, called *auricular acupuncture*, seems to work better than the other methods. One of the advantages of acupuncture is that there usually aren't any side effects. Sometimes there are changes in appetite, sleep patterns, or in your emotional state, but these pass very quickly.

> **Smoking Signals** _____
>
> **Auricular acupuncture** is a form of acupuncture that concentrates on the acupuncture points in the ears. In auricular acupuncture, the practitioner places needles around the ears. The needles cause the release of endorphins, which are the body's own natural "feel-good" chemicals. These endorphins are supposed to block the "feel-bad" chemicals of nicotine withdrawal.

The biggest problem with acupuncture is that, just like hypnosis, there is not a lot of good scientific evidence that it works for smoking cessation. In fact, the studies so far indicate that it doesn't work for most people. However, you know yourself best. So if you think your body might respond to this type of therapy, and you are able to find a reputable acupuncturist, go for it. Perhaps the best idea is to combine acupuncture with some other more traditional form of smoking cessation, such as the gum, pills, patches, or a class.

The Pros of Acupuncture

- No or minimal side effects
- Can be combined with other methods
- Has been around for 2,000 years

The Cons of Acupuncture

- Can be expensive
- Not typically covered by health insurance
- Slightly uncomfortable
- Lacking evidence of efficacy

Our advice: Although evidence is lacking, it may be a good choice to use in combination with another, better proven method.

Herbal Medicine

Herbs have been used for thousands of years to treat a variety of illnesses. There are only a handful of herbs that are used to specifically help people quit smoking. Some people swear that the spice Cream of Tartar, for instance, has helped them to quit. Some herbs are taken in the form of pills, while others are used as teas.

One big problem with herbs concerns their purity. Unlike prescription drugs, the FDA does not regulate herbs. This means that virtually anyone can sell herbs, and it also means that you don't have any reliable way to know if the product you buy is really what the label says it's supposed to be. The best advice is to talk to the owner of the store where you buy your herbs to find out more about the quality of the product you are thinking about buying. Also, try to stick to brand names that you know to be of good quality.

The Pros of Herbal Medicine

- Easy to get
- Doesn't involve a prescription

The Cons of Herbal Medicine

- Lacking evidence of efficacy
- Unknown purity
- May cause interactions when mixed with medications

Our advice: Lack of evidence, impurities, safety concerns, and possible interactions with medications make us leery of this method.

Aromatherapy

Aromatherapy involves inhaling fumes of various chemical mixtures. The aromas are supposed to help fight off cravings and other withdrawal symptoms. The exact way they accomplish this is unknown. The following is a commonly tried mixture.

Mix the essential oils as follows:

- Three parts lemon
- Two parts geranium
- One part everlast

The lemon is said to help detoxify the body, the geranium helps balance the hormones in your body, and the everlast is supposed to help your body fix any damage done by smoking.

The Pros of Aromatherapy

◆ Inexpensive

◆ Can be a relaxing ritual

◆ Easy to use

The Cons of Aromatherapy

◆ Not proven to work

Our advice: Again, just as is true for herbs, there isn't any real evidence that aromatherapy works. If you are interested in using it, we suggest that you combine it with a more traditional method. This unproven method may be a good add-on to a more traditional method.

The Power of Imagery

Imagery involves creating a strong image in your mind that you can use to overcome the desire to smoke a cigarette. For example, one image you could keep in mind to stave off the cravings is you as a very healthy, active nonsmoker. Focus on this image in your mind for 10 to 20 minutes, twice a day, so that it becomes something you can easily conjure up. When a desire to smoke comes, conjure up this image to overcome the desire.

This method also doesn't have any strong evidence showing that it's effective, but it can't hurt and it's free. We like to use it because it gives you a goal and helps you focus on the positive side of quitting. Also, if you can see yourself as a nonsmoker, it helps the quitting process no matter what method you are using.

The Pros of Imagery

◆ It's free

◆ Focuses on the positive side of quitting

◆ Keeps your eye on the goal

◆ Can help you to manage feelings of stress

The Cons of Imagery

◆ Not proven to work

Our advice: Another good add-on to a more traditional method.

Meditation

This is a very helpful method because it addresses one of the reasons most people who smoke continue to light up—relaxing and reducing stress. Remember, the nicotine is a powerful mood regulator that helps you relax when you are stressed out. Meditating also helps people relax, and its effects can last for many hours. There's really a lot to gain and nothing to lose by meditating.

Meditation is a great way to learn how to relax, and it's a good idea to add it onto whatever other method you decide to use. (Many quit-smoking classes will incorporate this into their stress management lesson.)

The Pros of Meditation

◆ Easy to learn

◆ Very relaxing

◆ Addresses the stress side of smoking

The Cons of Meditation

◆ Not a proven method

◆ Probably not enough when used alone

Our advice: We wouldn't suggest that you rely solely on meditation, but it's a great add-on tool.

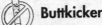 **Buttkicker** _____

There are several different forms of meditation; some are easy to learn, while others are more involved. One simple method begins by getting into a comfortable position. Try sitting on the floor on a comfortable cushion. You can even sit in a chair with your feet comfortably on the floor. Next, lower your eyes to a 45-degree angle and try not to stare at anything in particular. Once you feel comfortable, begin to take some gentle breaths of medium depth. As you are breathing, begin to count your breaths. One for every inhalation, two for every exhalation. Count up to 10 and then start all over again.

Don't focus on clearing your mind of any thoughts; just try to concentrate on the counting. If a thought comes into your mind, don't fight it. Just keep on counting. Practice this for up to 10 to 20 minutes each day. Try not to worry about whether you're doing it right. With practice, you will begin to feel relaxed for longer periods of time.

Future Trends

One of the most exciting things on the quit-smoking horizon is a quit-smoking vaccine. The vaccine teaches your body to produce substances that latch onto any nicotine in your bloodstream. This imprisons the nicotine and prevents it from attaching to the receptors in your brain. Currently, it's still experimental.

Lots More

There are many, many other "alternative" ways to help you quit smoking. In fact, there are new methods that come out virtually every day. Some are legitimate attempts to help you quit, while others are legitimate attempts at cleaning out your wallet. Use your best judgment and think about what might be right for you.

What we've discovered about these methods is that their effectiveness largely depends upon the person trying to quit smoking. Sure, we like to use quit-smoking medications combined with structured group programs because there is a lot of good evidence out there that shows these methods work. But we also like to use some less traditional methods. In most cases, we suggest a combination method. For example, we think it's a great idea to use nicotine patches, Bupropion, hypnosis, and acupuncture, while attending a support group. But then again, we have been accused of being obsessed with helping people quit smoking. Again, it all depends on the individual needs, goals, and personality of the person involved.

There are 45 million smokers in the United States, and that means there are about 45 million different ways to quit smoking. Just talk to anybody who has successfully quit, and you will hear a personal rendition of what worked. The point of the matter is that there is no one best way to quit. If there were, everyone would use it. (Actually, this book is by far the best method ever created, and we really don't see any reason why there should be anything else out there!)

The Least You Need to Know

♦ There is no one best way to quit smoking, so use your judgment and decide what will work best for you.

♦ Hard evidence is lacking that any of the "alternative" methods can help you quit smoking.

♦ Hypnosis, acupuncture, herbs, aromatherapy, and imagery may work better when combined with a more traditional method.

♦ There may be a stop-smoking vaccine available in the near future.

♦ When hearing about a new method, hold on to your wallet, and use your best judgment.

The Seven-Day Countdown to Q-Day

In This Chapter

♦ Complete special activities that will get you pumped up and ready for quit day

♦ Find out how to avoid some of the most common mistakes of quitting smoking

♦ Fine-tune your motivation

♦ Strengthen your commitment to becoming a nonsmoker

As you can tell by the title, you really shouldn't read this chapter until you are seven days from your quit date. We've written it especially to help get you prepared and pumped up for your exciting quit day. If you're still more than one week away from quitting by the time you reach this section of the book, try to wait to read it. Whatever you do, be sure to save this section of the book for your actual journey to Quitsville.

A bit later in the chapter, you'll find a new "Buttkicker" activity. You should read the rest of this chapter on the date you've written next to "Q Day-7," one week before your quit date. You may even want to pencil those dates into the margins throughout the rest of this chapter. There is a specific activity that you are asked to complete on each and every day this week. And remember that we asked you to keep an open mind. Just go along with us!

Day Seven—Commit to Quit: Getting the Word Out

It's time to ring the bells and sound the alarms—your quit day is only a week away! By fighting the natural tendency to want to keep this whole quit thing "hush-hush," you will be able to solidify and strengthen your commitment by telling people about your quit date. Although there may be a few individuals worth bypassing, most people will be thrilled to hear your good news and will gleefully cheer you on. So, call them, fax them, write them, or e-mail them—get the word out about your exciting new project any way that you can!

Buttkicker

Beginning with your actual quit date, fill in the dates for the week leading up to your big day. As you read through this chapter, you will be given specific activities to do on each of the days.

Day	Date Example
Q Day (Quit Day)	Wednesday, July 4
Q Day–1	Tuesday, July 3
Q Day–2	Monday, July 2
Q Day–3	Sunday, July 1
Q Day–4	Saturday, June 30
Q Day–5	Friday, June 29
Q Day–6	Thursday, June 28
Q Day–7	Wednesday, June 27

Remember, you can notify the people on your list in a variety of ways. You can use the phone or tell them face-to-face. You might even want to get creative and hand out homemade flyers, cards, or banners; some print the announcement in the local paper! Now that's commitment!

Day Six—A Jar of Kick-Butt

Think back to those fun little science projects you used to do in school. Well, it's time for another one! As of today, don't throw out any of your cigarette butts. That's right—for one short week, we are asking you to collect all of those ashtray butts and put them in some sort of glass jar, like a mayonnaise jar.

Many people are surprised to see just how many yucky little butts they accumulate on a daily basis. In fact, most people who smoke don't want to see how many butts they create each day, so they empty their ashtrays on a regular basis, keeping them sparkling clean. The psychology behind this phenomenon is a good example of basic human nature: If I keep those ashtrays clean, I won't have to think about what I'm doing to my lungs and the rest of my body.

This butt jar will be used as part of a simple, yet very effective, aversion technique. If you have any doubts, just play along with us. It's really quite easy. We'll be using this little kick-butt jar later, so hang onto it! Six days and counting ...

Day Five—Cutting Down or Beefing Up?

Now you're five days away from your first day as a nonsmoker. By the way, if you're experiencing anxiety instead of cheer, don't worry. You're normal! Just stay focused on the activities planned for each day this week.

We have three options for you at this point. For the next five days, you may choose to smoke as usual, decrease your level of smoking, or increase it. You need to decide which option is best for you. Because you've committed to a quit date in five days, it really doesn't matter too much which way you go. Just select the option that feels the best for you right now.

Although some people will choose the first option—continuing to smoke your usual amount right up until the evening before your quit date—most will actually go with the second or third option.

Cutting Down

Option two involves cutting down gradually, so that you smoke less each day. This method is called *nicotine fading*. The principle behind it is that you will gradually decrease the nicotine level in your blood, which should make quitting easier. The reality is that as you cut down on the number of cigarettes smoked, your brain instructs your body to extract more nicotine out of each cigarette. This is done (without your knowing it) by inhaling a bit more deeply, holding each puff in your lungs a split second longer, or taking more puffs off of each cigarette. The end result is that the nicotine level in your blood remains amazingly constant, even if you've cut down from 40 cigarettes to 10 per day!

> **Smoking Signals**
>
> **Nicotine fading** is a method by which a quitter gradually decreases the number of cigarettes smoked until he or she has quit. This technique allows for a gradual reduction in the amount of nicotine in your blood so as to avoid withdrawal symptoms.

However, that's not to say that option two doesn't have any benefit. In fact, it can be quite helpful. The benefit of cutting down in preparation for your quit day is that it gives you a head start because you get to practice not smoking in specific situations. For example, you may choose to cut out the cigarette you have with coffee or the one you smoke in the car on the way to work. That's one less cigarette you'll have to think about when you finally quit.

Some people choose to tackle their toughest challenge now by eliminating the cigarette that is the hardest to give up. For many people, this is the first cigarette of the morning or the last one at night. Although we recommend going for the easiest ones at this point, you can also tackle that one big challenge to get some practice. The idea is to try substituting a different, healthier behavior. Or you can try to distract yourself when you get the urge.

If you are worried or feeling anxious about your impending quit date, we recommend option two. It will help you prepare for your quit date by actually beginning to take action, which should alleviate some of your anxiety.

Smoke 'Em All Up

Option three is for you to actually increase your smoking. Yes, that's right: smoke more than ever for the next five days. Unless your doctor has told you that you must stop smoking right away for a medical reason, it's okay to do this. The natural tendency for many people is to smoke more than usual right before quit day because they want to finish all of the cigarettes they've stocked up on (wouldn't want to waste any) or because they're concerned about "giving up" their one pleasure in life.

Although it's okay to smoke a little extra for the next few days, it's also important to recognize that you really aren't "giving up" anything. In fact, it's imperative that you focus on what you will be gaining: good health, easier breathing, fresher breath, freedom from a controlling addiction, more money in your pocket, and so on.

Smoke Alarm

Don't focus on the "I'm giving up something" side of quitting. While it's true that you are giving up something that you may enjoy doing, there are many more things that you will be gaining instead. It's all in the way you look at it.

So recite your five most important reasons to quit every time you hear yourself thinking or talking about "giving up" cigarettes. In fact, you need to take the phrase "giving up" completely out of your vocabulary. Your words have tremendous power over how you feel and think, so when you catch yourself saying "giving up," make a correction and say "getting healthier." And don't worry, because in just two days you will begin to focus on adding more joy and fun into your life.

Day Four—Money to Burn on the Good Things in Life

Notice how much money you'll save each day once you've quit smoking.

> **Buttkicker** _____
>
> Write down the amount of money you will save from quitting:
>
> Each day: $_____
>
> Each week: $_____
>
> Now think of ways to spend (or save) that money (there's a list below that can help spur your imagination!)
>
> Each day: _____
>
> Each week: _____

The Good Things in Life

As human beings, many of our decisions in life are guided by what is known as the pleasure principle. In other words, if it feels good, we are likely to continue doing "it"; if it feels bad (physically or mentally), we are less likely to keep doing it or to try it again.

In order to quit smoking successfully, it's important to make the process of quitting, and life thereafter, as positive and pleasurable as possible. That's why social and behavioral scientists tell us that it's important to plan, and follow through with, a system of rewards. In other words, you must include things that feel good and make you happy in your quit plan.

The fact that you will save lots of money when you quit smoking ties in nicely with the need to feel good, to enjoy the good things in life. You will have some extra cash on hand that you will be able to use toward your rewards.

Let's start by identifying some things that make you feel good or happy—things that are fun or relaxing. Amazingly enough, some people have a difficult time coming up with this list. Here are some ideas suggested by ex-smokers we've talked with:

- Rent one of your favorite comedies from the video store.

- Call or write a letter to an out-of-town friend or family member you haven't talked with in a while.

- Schedule a dental cleaning right after your quit date.

- Pick or purchase a bouquet of fresh flowers.

- Go for a refreshing walk by the beach, around the lake, or through the park.

- Buy a new tape or CD.

- Take a relaxing bubble bath.

- Get a massage.

- Go to that movie you've been meaning to see.

- Plan a trip to someplace you've never been.

- Join a hobby club and meet new people who are interested in the same things you are.

- Sign up for a class to learn to do something you've always had an interest in, such as horseback riding, playing the guitar, or dance lessons.

- Get a manicure or pedicure.

- Get a new pet and give it lots of love.

- Complete this sentence: "One of these days, I'm going to _____." Now go do it!

The general principle behind using rewards is that when positive things are tied to specific goals, you are more likely to accomplish your goal. The key is that the reward must be contingent upon reaching the goal (such as staying smoke-free for 24 hours). Avoid using activities that you're going to do no matter what as rewards.

Rewards are also more effective when you reward yourself as soon as you can after you reach your goal. So, most of your rewards should be "short-term" rewards to which you can treat yourself within 24 hours of accomplishing your goal.

Buttkicker

Write down a list of at least six rewards. Make sure your list includes mostly short-term rewards and a couple of more long-term rewards.

1. _____
2. _____
3. _____
4. _____
5. _____
6. _____

Now circle the one that you will give yourself for making it through your first 24 hours without smoking. Make sure it's a really good one that you can treat yourself to right away!

Day Three—Preparing Your Environment

You might be surprised to find out just how much your physical environment has been set up to support your tobacco addiction.

Use this checklist to go through your home, office, and car and remove the (now) offensive items:

- ❏ Lighters and matches

- ❏ Ashtrays (all of them)

- ❏ Breath mints and gum

- ❏ Tobacco company T-shirts, caps, or other items

- ❏ Clothing with burned holes in them

- ❏ Loose cigarettes or packs in your glove box, under the car seat, in drawers, and so on

Collect all of these items and set them aside for your quit date.

Day Two—Focusing on the Goal

In the halls and boardrooms of big businesses, you will often hear the term cost-benefit analysis. Cost-benefit analysis is when you figure out the costs versus the benefits of doing an activity. Now it's time to figure out the cost-benefit analysis of continuing to smoke versus quitting for good.

Buttkicker

Carefully fill in the following chart in detail with complete and utter honesty. The benefits and costs can be in terms of finances (money saved or money spent), how you feel (pleasure, sadness, or joy), or anything else you can think of. Take your time doing this activity because it will help you clearly see why you are quitting.

Benefits of Continuing	Benefits of Quitting
Costs of Continuing	**Costs of Quitting**

Day One—Twenty-Four Hours and Counting!

Congratulations! Tomorrow is your big day! Go through the following checklist to make sure that you are ready for this exciting and rewarding adventure.

Preparation Checklist for Quit Day

❑ Collected ALL cigarettes, lighters, ashtrays, and so on.

❑ Memorized your top five reasons to quit.

❑ Informed at least two people about your quit date and asked for their support.

❑ Talked with your doctor or pharmacist about nicotine replacement products or other quit-smoking medications.

❑ Picked out a quit-smoking class to attend.

❑ Decided whether or not to use herbs, meditation, or hypnosis.

❑ Found your positive attitude and plugged it in.

Saying Good-Bye and Good Riddance

Now it's time to say good-bye and good riddance to your cigarettes. Many people find that their cigarettes have become their companions—their best friends of sorts. That's because that trusty cigarette with its nicotine effects and familiar ritual is always there. It's there when you're feeling sad, when you're happy, when you're lonely, when you're celebrating, or when you're upset or angry.

Pack Facts

Many people are surprised to find how emotionally attached they've become to their cigarettes. In fact, some people don't realize this until the day they quit.

Chances are that you have learned to rely on your cigarettes more than you realize for emotional comfort and companionship. But the truth of the matter is that true friends would never treat you the way this drug delivery device does. So it's time to bid those cigarettes adieu, and to do it in writing. This is a very important activity that only takes about 10 minutes, so don't skip it!

As you complete the Good-bye and Good Riddance letter, you may find yourself feeling both relieved and anxious. This is normal because the logical side of your brain (that has your best interest at heart) is thrilled beyond belief that you are about to get rid of this poison. On the other hand, the addiction-based voice within is terrified that this time, you really mean it. It's terrified that you're about to put this addiction to rest for good.

Buttkicker

On a separate sheet of paper, copy the following phrases; then complete each sentence with the first thoughts that pop into your head.

Dear Cigarettes,

You seemed like a friend in many ways. Some of the things you've done for me are _____.
But over the years, I realized that you are not a friend at all. Some of the things you've done to me are _____, and a real friend would NEVER do that. It's time I stop thinking about you and start thinking about me. I deserve to be healthy and free from this addiction that has been stealing my _____. And it's also time for me to start thinking about others around me. What you've done to them is _____.
So I bid you adieu. It's my turn to take charge, and only I will have the last laugh. Good-bye and good riddance to you.

Signed: _____ Date: _____

Now that you've completed this week's worth of preparation activities and you've gone over the checklist, you can rest easy. Just relax and get a good night's sleep. Tomorrow is the day you take full control.

The Least You Need to Know

- Let key people know you are quitting.

- Cutting down a little bit now can help you practice not smoking.

- Review your reasons for quitting.

- Think about enjoyable things to replace smoking.

- Figuring out your cost-benefit analysis helps clarify your reasons for quitting.

- Complete your preparation quit list.

Chapter 5

Ready, Set, Go! It's Time to Kick Butt!

In This Chapter

- Step into the tobacco-free world
- Master staying smoke-free for the first 24 hours
- Quitting with a smoker in your house
- Preventing and managing urges and cravings
- Act and react differently

Well, here you are. It's the big day you've been gearing up for. It's your quit day. Congratulations! In this chapter, we will give you everything else that you need to make it through the first 24 hours as a nonsmoker. We suggest that you read through this chapter at the very beginning of your first smoke-free 24-hour period (or the evening before).

It's extremely important to realize that the first 24 hours sets the tone for the remainder of your quit program. So we want you to savor every word of this chapter (like a big, thick, juicy steak) and then implement it. Put it to use, and do whatever it takes to remain completely tobacco-free for the next 24 hours. You can do it, just like millions and millions of others. Today really is the first day of the rest of your healthy, tobacco-free life, so let's get started!

It's Quitting Time

We're going to ask you to answer a series of questions throughout the next few chapters. The purpose of these questions, called *check-in stations*, will be for you to assess and acknowledge how you are doing and how you are feeling each day. It will also give you a record that you can use to monitor your progress and to see when things are beginning to slip out of your hands a bit. And if things begin to slip a little, don't worry.

 Buttkicker

Check-In Station

On a scale of 1 to 10, with a 10 being the best, most comfortable and a 1 being the worst, most miserable, how would you rate yourself at this time:

1. How comfortable are you about not smoking for the next 24 hours? ___

   1 = Extremely uncomfortable and worried. 10 = Extremely comfortable; no concerns.

2. How motivated are you to quit smoking for good? ___

   1 = Not motivated at all; I'm going to throw this book into the garbage. 10 = Extremely motivated; I'll do whatever it takes.

3. How confident are you that you will remain smoke-free for the next 24 hours? ___

   1 = I'm sure I won't make it. 10 = I know that I will stay quit.

4. What specific situation do you think will be your greatest challenge for the next 24 hours? _____

5. What are your plans of action for this situation (Plans A, B, and C)? _____

6. How troublesome are your withdrawal symptoms, such as cravings, nervousness, difficulty concentrating, and so on? ___

   1 = Overwhelming and miserable. 10 = Completely comfortable; no discomfort.

Commit to Quit: The Gear Dump

Take out the Good-Bye and Good Riddance letter you wrote to your cigarettes in the last chapter. Read it out loud to yourself (or to your cigarettes). Now it's time to get rid of all of those extra cigarettes, ash-trays, hole-burnt clothes, lighters, matches, etc. Take out that box or bag you set aside, and dump all of your tobacco-related items into it. This may sound strange, but pour enough water, syrup, glue, or some other yucky substance all over the contents. Close it off, say good-bye, and dump it in the trash. You've taken the biggest step so far!

Now it's time for some commitment. We had a couple of attorneys draw up the following "Commit to Quit Contract." There isn't any fine print (except for the part where we get your house and car), and it's pretty straightforward. Basically, we are asking that you just make a commitment to remain smoke-free for the next 24 hours.

Buttkicker
24 Hour Commit to Quit Contract

I promise to do whatever it takes to remain smoke-free for the next 24 hours. From now until __ o'clock on _____, I will handle each craving a new way because I know that I'm only a puff away from a pack a day. The reward that I will give to myself for accomplishing this feat is _____ _____.

Signed: _____   Date: _____

Quitting with a Smoker in Your House

If you share your household with someone who smokes, don't fret. There are strategies that can help both of you get through this quit attempt as a team.

First of all, acknowledge that everyone has to quit on his or her schedule, when he or she is ready. Although it would be great to quit as a team, your smoking family member(s) can still be supportive of your efforts even if he or she continues to smoke. Have a little heart to heart with him or her. Say something like, "I know you aren't ready to quit, and that's okay. I wouldn't have been ready last month. But I would really appreciate your support. As you know, quitting is going to be difficult, but with your help, I know I can do it."

At this point, your family member should be feeling less threatened by your intention to quit and should be ready to hear how he or she can help. Ask your partner to please keep all cigarettes, matches, ashtrays, etc., out of sight because these are powerful triggers that bring on extra urges (and who needs that?). Then decide where smoking will occur and where it will not. Some of the options (from most desirable to least) include:

◆ All smoking takes place outside of the home.

◆ Indoor smoking is permitted in one room only.

◆ At least one room remains a smoke-free zone.

You can assure your partner that this is a temporary adjustment that will really help you to get through the first few challenging weeks.

Taming the Craving

The first step to taking full control over your nicotine cravings and desires is to understand how they come about. Over the years, your body has grown accustomed to a certain level of nicotine. In fact, it relies on that level to feel good. As long as your blood level stays within this nicotine comfort zone, everything is cool. But, if you don't smoke enough, your blood level will go below the nicotine comfort zone and you will experience cravings and withdrawal symptoms.

Think about how you smoke. Most likely, your smoking pattern (how often you smoke and how many cigarettes you smoke) keeps your body within its nicotine comfort zone. For example, you probably have a cigarette every hour or two, which allows you to continuously replenish your nicotine level, keeping it high enough to avoid cravings and withdrawal. If you were to spread out your smoking to every six hours, the nicotine level would fall and you would get cravings. Cravings are your body's way of letting you know that you are out of your nicotine comfort zone.

If you've chosen to use a nicotine replacement medication, you will automatically be able to minimize any withdrawal symptoms and certainly take the edge off of your cravings. That's because the medication keeps your blood levels of nicotine within your nicotine comfort zone. By slowly weaning off the medication, your body grows accustomed to lower levels of nicotine.

However, even if you have chosen to use one of the nicotine replacement medications, you will still need a plan to address the psychological and habitual components of why you smoke. The cravings that occur for these reasons are unaffected by medications, and that's why your quit plan needs to include nonmedication strategies for dealing with them. And if you've chosen to go forward without any medications whatsoever, you will need to have a plan that addresses the physical, psychological, and habitual urges and cravings.

Cravings only last about five minutes or so, whether you light up or not. In the first few days of quitting, you may find yourself bombarded with one craving after another. The good news is that these cravings soon become less intense, shorter in duration, and less frequent.

In other words, after the first couple of days of quitting, you will have fewer cravings each day, until you find yourself almost never having any. The intense, almost overpowering desire to smoke that you experience in the early stages will soon become much less intense, almost insignificant, with time. And the cravings that may last five minutes (or longer) in the beginning will last for only a few seconds, like a fleeting thought. Now that's good news!

Now that you understand how and why the physical cravings for nicotine occur, we need to put together a plan for managing them. As with many other things in life, the best way to handle this challenge is to avoid it. If you've chosen not to make use of any of these quit smoking aids, you will need a strong plan for handling these cravings, which often pop up quickly and without warning. And to make matters more confusing, there are also the psychological and habitual desires for a cigarette, which many people confuse with physical cravings. Either way, a solid plan will boost your chances for success.

The Tools of Prevention

At this point it is very important for you to set aside your reservations and pre-judgments. Remember that we've asked you to put some faith in us and to just "play along." Keep your mind open and try these strategies before deciding whether or not each one will have value. You will be pleasantly surprised to find out that some of the strategies that seemed silly or overly simple were actually instrumental in helping you to successfully get through your first 24 hours without a single puff.

HALT in the Name of the Law!

One of the best ways to manage your urges to smoke is to avoid them. You can do this by remembering the acronym H.A.L.T. Try not to let yourself get too hungry, angry, lonely, or tired. These are all triggers to smoke, and you will have more cravings to deal with if you allow yourself to get into any one of these states. Rather than telling you what not to do (we'll leave that for your mother), let's take a look at what you should be doing in order to avoid these situations.

In order to avoid hunger, be sure to have frequent healthy snacks. We suggest a small, healthy snack every two or three hours, coupled with a big glass of cold water.

As far as getting angry goes, just try to avoid frustrating situations for the first couple of days. If you do find yourself feeling angry or upset about something, you need to express those feelings right away in a positive way. You can write down your concerns or call a supportive friend to talk it over. Just be sure not to let your anger get bottled up inside.

A good way to avoid feeling lonely is to plan some fun activities with friends if at all possible. When that isn't possible, plan on going to a nonsmoking environment sure to be full of people, such as the park, the movies, or even the grocery store. Just get out of the house.

Feeling tired. Now there's one you should know how to avoid. Just be sure to get plenty of sleep and rest. These are two different things, so be sure to plan for both. Go to bed early and plan a break during your day to take a nap or to practice a relaxation technique.

Scrambling Your Eggs and Your Days

For the next few days, you should try to scramble things up—and not just your eggs. What that means is that we want you to do things completely different than usual. Most people establish a routine that helps them to stay organized and on schedule. Routines help us to become efficient. Unfortunately, the behavior of smoking has become intertwined with your daily routines. So, in order to break those habit patterns, we want you to completely forget about being efficient for a few days. Go from being Felix Unger to Oscar Madison.

Scramble up your day in every way that you can. Do things out of order. Change things. Skip things. Alter everything you can think of in your daily routine and your physical environment. If you usually walk to work, ride your bike instead. If you always have two cups of coffee, cut back to one or add another. Try a new place for lunch. Join a gym. You need to think and feel different for a few days. This will not only break up your smoking routines, but it will also help you to prevent a variety of cravings and urges.

Tools for Taming Cravings

The model that we recommend for taming your cravings and handling other types of urges to smoke is very straightforward. It's also very effective when used consistently. In a nutshell, you need to blast each craving to smoke as soon as it arises with two types of techniques. We call this our double-whammy approach. One is a cognitive strategy, or a thought process. The other is a behavioral strategy, or an action. Give each craving the ol' 1-2, and you'll see yourself conquer one urge after another. You'll be the Muhammad Ali of craving conquerors.

Cognitive Strategies: Slogans and Affirmations

Nicotine has been doing a number on your brain, and you've been playing lots of mind games in order to permit yourself to continue smoking. Now it's time to take that good brain power of yours and turn it around so that it works for you instead of against you.

When a craving or desire to smoke arises, and you hear that little voice within trying to talk you into having just one, that's the time to break out your cognitive strategy. That's the time when you will need to have a strong, solid answer ready for that little voice.

Your cognitive strategy can be reciting your five most important reasons to quit, or repeating a personal slogan or affirmation. These are some we've heard from successful ex-smokers:

- I'm only a puff away from a pack a day.

- This craving will go away whether I smoke or not.

- Deciding to quit is one of the smartest things I've ever done.

- I will breathe easier, live longer, and enjoy a better quality of life without cigarettes.

- No matter what, smoking is not an option.

- I'm in control now, and I choose health and freedom.

- One is never enough, and any more than that is too many.

You can use one of these or create your own. The more positive statements you have, the better. Some people say the statement to themselves, others say it out loud. Try it both ways, and see which works best for you. The point is that *you must have a positive statement rehearsed and ready to go when the urge hits.*

Behavioral Strategies: Taking Action

The reality is that you simply can't avoid all cravings. That brings us to the other half of the double-whammy approach, which is the action that you choose to take when the craving happens. The options are endless, but here are a few of the most popular behavioral strategies that successful ex-smokers have used:

- Performing deep-breathing exercises

- Going for a walk

- Chewing gum

- Singing a favorite song

- Having a healthy snack

- Going somewhere else (anywhere else, even into another room)

- Taking a shower

- Brushing your teeth (10 times a day is fine!)

- Calling a friend

- Re-reading a section of this book

- Rewriting your reasons to quit

- Writing a letter

- Drinking water (try adding cloves, mint leaves, or lemon for variety)

What you want to do is use the best behavioral strategy for each situation. But just in case a strategy doesn't work, you need to have a Plan B and a Plan C. In other words, if you find that going for a walk isn't quite getting rid of that urge, try singing out loud or calling your friend.

At this point, you need to review your trigger situations so that you can anticipate where cravings are likely to occur. Then you will plug in two or three strategies for each situation. We've listed some of the more common triggers to smoke in the following section, and we've included some excellent strategies for each one. You can try our ideas or create your own. The idea is to do things differently. Choose one and check it off for your Plans A, B, and C.

My Strategic Plan for Overcoming Cravings

Trigger	Plan A	Plan B	Plan C
Suggested strategies			
Waking up			
◆ Shower immediately	_____	_____	_____
◆ Sleep in	_____	_____	_____
◆ Go for a walk	_____	_____	_____
◆ Your choice	_____	_____	_____
Morning coffee			
◆ Switch to juice, tea, or decaf	_____	_____	_____
◆ Drink in a different place	_____	_____	_____
◆ Hold mug in the opposite hand	_____	_____	_____
◆ Your choice	_____	_____	_____
Driving to work			
◆ Take an alternate route	_____	_____	_____
◆ Listen to a different radio station or CD	_____	_____	_____
◆ Chew gum	_____	_____	_____
During breaks			
◆ Go for a walk	_____	_____	_____
◆ Have a healthy snack	_____	_____	_____
◆ Hang out with a different group	_____	_____	_____

Trigger	Plan A	Plan B	Plan C
Suggested strategies			
After work			
◆ Drink water	_____	_____	_____
◆ Healthy snack	_____	_____	_____
◆ Deep breathing	_____	_____	_____
After meals			
◆ Chew gum	_____	_____	_____
◆ Call a friend	_____	_____	_____
◆ Go for a walk	_____	_____	_____
With friends who smoke			
◆ Avoid this situation for a while if possible	_____	_____	_____
◆ Ask them to support you by not smoking around you for a little while	_____	_____	_____
◆ If they light up, make up an excuse to leave for a few minutes	_____	_____	_____
Before bedtime			
◆ Write a letter	_____	_____	_____
◆ Drink water, warm milk, or caffeine-free tea	_____	_____	_____
◆ Call a friend	_____	_____	_____

We suggest that you photocopy this page so that you can adjust your plan every 24 hours at first. After the first week, you can adjust it weekly. It's important to always think ahead and plan. Don't just try to wing it—chances are, that's what tripped you up in the past.

The Least You Need to Know

◆ The first 24 hours are key: No matter what, smoking is not an option.

◆ Get rid of all your cigarettes.

◆ Combine a cognitive strategy (positive thought or personal slogan) with a behavioral strategy (do something different) to take control of urges.

◆ HALT! Never get too hungry, angry, lonely, or tired.

◆ Cravings only last a few minutes—then they go away, whether you light up or not.

◆ You are only a puff away from a pack a day.

Chapter 6

The Twenty-Four-Hour Check-In

In This Chapter

- Adjusting your 24-hour plan
- Reviewing the benefits of quitting
- Starting your Cash Stash
- Getting your reward
- Troubleshooting the next 24 hours
- Making your second commitment contract

As you've discovered by now, the first 24 hours after you stop smoking is a real eye-opener. You've probably learned a lot about how well prepared you were to quit and what may or may not have been missing from your plan. However, even though the first 24 hours are quite important, you're still practicing at quitting smoking. By looking at what worked and didn't work, you can easily make adjustments for the next day.

In this chapter, we focus on the importance of recognizing your achievements so far. It's crucial that you track your progress and reward yourself each day for at least the next few weeks. Keeping up your motivation is a key ingredient for success. Let's get started.

Congratulations, You Survived!

Welcome back! It's been 24 hours since you began your Quit Day, and we can't wait to hear how you're doing! We're willing to bet that you made it—and without a single puff. How do we know? Because you got rid of all of your cigarettes, you arranged for social support, you learned strategies for staying quit, and you wrote out your strategic plan beforehand. All of that spells out S-U-C-C-E-S-S. (Actually, it spells out "ralw," but that's not a word.)

Now don't get us wrong; we know it hasn't exactly been a piece of cake. In fact, you may be wondering how in the world you are going to make it through the *next* 24 hours. The answer is, "one day (or one hour) at a time." Just keep applying the strategies that have been working for you so far, one hour at a time, situation by situation, and you will get another day as a nonsmoker under your belt.

In the meantime, it's essential that you recognize every cigarette that you haven't smoked in the last 24 hours. Each cigarette you've passed up is making you stronger and stronger. You are doing such a great job! Let's do the formal check-in before we go to the next step (see the following Buttkicker).

After you've checked in, let's take a look at your Buttkicker scores:

♦ Your level of comfort (Question #1) may have dropped down much lower from its level 24 hours ago. This is normal, and you will see it go back up over the next few days or so.

♦ Your motivation (Question #2) should still be high, hopefully 8 or above.

♦ Your confidence (Question #3) should be a point or two higher than it was 24 hours ago.

♦ Your greatest challenge for the next few days (Questions #4 and #5) should be identified and you should have several plans of action to meet it.

◆ If you are using one of the quit-smoking medications, you will still be having withdrawal symptoms, but they will be a lot milder than if you weren't. Your score will be in the 6 to 10 range. If you are not using a quit-smoking medication, your withdrawal symptoms will most likely be very strong. Chances are your score falls in the 1 to 4 range.

 Buttkicker
Check-In Station

On a scale of 1 to 10, with a 10 being the best, most comfortable and a 1 being the worst, most miserable, how would you rate yourself at this time:

1. How comfortable are you about not smoking for the next 24 hours? ___

1 = Extremely uncomfortable and worried. 10 = Extremely comfortable; no concerns.

2. How motivated are you to quit smoking for good? ___

1 = Not motivated at all; I'm going to throw this book into the garbage. 10 = Extremely motivated; I'll do whatever it takes.

3. How confident are you that you will remain smoke-free for the next 24 hours? ___

1 = I'm sure I won't make it. 10 = I know that I will stay quit.

4. What specific situation do you think will be your greatest challenge for the next 24 hours? _____

5. What are your plans of action for this situation (Plans A, B, and C)? _____

6. How troublesome are your withdrawal symptoms, such as cravings, nervousness, difficulty concentrating, and so on? ___

1 = Overwhelming and miserable. 10 = Completely comfortable; no discomfort.

Recognize and Celebrate Your Success

It is extremely important that you recognize and celebrate each day of success. Every challenging situation that you manage to get through without the use of cigarettes is a victory, and you must recognize and celebrate them.

In order to help you do this, we would like you to maintain a special smoke-free calendar. It will help you chart and recognize your progress. You can use a wall calendar or copy our "Calendar of Success."

 Buttkicker

Charting Your Progress: Your Calendar of Success

At the end of each smoke-free day, draw a happy face or some other symbol of your success. Place a "Q" on your quit day (day one) now.

	Mon	Tues	Wed	Thur	Fri	Sat	Sun
Week 1							
Week 2							
Week 3							
Week 4							
Week 5							

Withdrawal and the Process of Recovery

Withdrawal symptoms are very real, and they are likely to be your greatest challenge right now. Remember two things: They are temporary, and they will probably get worse before they get better. (We don't sugar coat this stuff, do we?)

Withdrawal symptoms are temporary because your body is learning (and remembering) how to get along without nicotine. It doesn't take your body too long to do this because nicotine was never supposed to be in your body to begin with. That's why we (and many others) prefer to refer to these symptoms as a recovery process.

If you're using Bupropion or a nicotine replacement therapy, your withdrawal symptoms should be less severe. However, that doesn't mean you don't need to do anything about them. Here are some strategies for dealing with some of the more common symptoms of withdrawal that you may find yourself experiencing in the upcoming week:

- ◆ **Drowsiness.** Go for a brisk walk every day, or get extra sleep by going to bed earlier.

- ◆ **Constipation.** Drink more water and juice; eat bran, fresh fruits, and veggies (like carrots); or go for a walk every day.

- ◆ **Difficulty concentrating.** Try to do fewer things for a while, go for frequent short walks, or try relaxation breathing.

- ◆ **Nervousness.** Practice relaxation techniques, or perform deep breathing or positive self-statements.

- ◆ **Sadness or depression.** Talk with someone who cares about you, get regular physical activity, or talk with your doctor if it persists for more than two weeks or feels overwhelming.

- ◆ **Constant cravings.** Remind yourself that a craving goes away in a few minutes whether you light up or not; make sure that you are not too hungry, angry, lonely, or tired; or distract yourself whenever a craving hits.

- ◆ **Irritability.** Get regular exercise, take time to do something fun, or rent one of your favorite funny movies.

- ◆ **Difficulty sleeping.** Drink warm milk before going to bed; don't exercise late in the day, but do exercise earlier in the day; read our book as a sure way to fall asleep in five minutes; or get out of bed for a little while.

Note: All of these symptoms are temporary and they will go away. However, if you are still irritable two months from now, you can't blame nicotine withdrawal.

If you are finding it difficult to function at work, consider taking some time off, or at least give yourself some more free time during the day. The best thing about the recovery process is that the symptoms will quickly become less frequent, less intense, and will occur less often. (We promise!)

In fact, if you find yourself feeling tempted to have "just one puff," remind yourself that doing this will only re-ignite the symptoms of withdrawal, making it harder for you to get to the comfortable stage.

Benefits of Quitting: The First Twenty-Four Hours

Isn't it great to know that your body is already recovering from tobacco poisoning? Some of the benefits your body is already experiencing include:

- More oxygen going to your brain and other organs
- You are taking control over the addiction
- Carbon monoxide levels drop
- Blood pressure and pulse rate decrease to normal
- Reduced risk of "sudden-death" heart attack

In the next few days, you will also experience these benefits:

- Walking becomes easier
- Overall energy increases
- Bronchial tubes relax and breathing becomes easier
- Food tastes and smells better
- Shortness of breath decreases

Urge Management in a Nutshell

There are some basic approaches that seem to work well for getting people through their first week smoke-free. Remember, your first week is your foundation for your smoke-free future, so pay close attention!

Avoid the Situation

Obviously you cannot go through life avoiding every situation that may trigger you to want to light up—but you can for a little while! In fact, we highly recommend avoidance of high-risk situations for the first week or two. Examples include bars, parties, breaks at work, and basically anything else that involves other smokers and/or alcohol.

Now, we know that this might go against your personal take-the-bull-by-the-horns style. In fact, you may be thinking something like, "Hey, I'm going to have to deal with this problem some time, so I might as well do it now." Our response to this is "You're right—partially." You *will* have to face these tough situations some time, but NOT NOW! We want you to increase your odds of getting through your first week without a puff. So, as the expert coaches that you've hired, listen to us. Avoid as many of these situations as you possibly can for just a little while, okay?

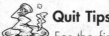 **Quit Tips**

For the first few weeks, avoid high-risk situations that might tempt you to smoke.

Leaving the Scene of an Urge

This is one of our favorite strategies for kicking your craving's butt. Whenever you find yourself in a situation that presents you with an overwhelming desire to smoke, just get the %$#@ out of there! It works! Again, this won't become your permanent way of going through life; it's just for a little while.

Alter the Environment

If you find yourself trapped in an unavoidable situation, get creative and do whatever you can to change things. (Remember the scrambling up your day concept?) For example, if you are driving to work and you get a craving, try changing the radio station or taking a different route so you will have to concentrate more. If you are at a friend's birthday party and it seems as though everyone around you is smoking, try moving to a different room, or start talking to someone who isn't smoking. Say you are at a dinner party and you find yourself wanting to smoke after you've finished eating. To overcome the craving, you could try drinking a beverage that's different than your usual, chewing gum, or brushing your teeth.

Ask for Support

Sometimes people relapse by themselves, but usually it's in the company of others. Practice assertive communication, and ask other people for their support by giving them specific suggestions of how they can be most helpful to you. For example, ask your friends not to smoke in front of you or to offer you any cigarettes. Explain to others that you are trying to quit and that it would be of great help if they support your effort.

> **Quit Tips**
>
> Getting the people around you to support you is a good way to avoid relapsing. However, they can only help you if you let them know what you are trying to do. Take it one step further and give them specific examples of how they can help you.

Standardize Your Action Plan

Remember that a strong plan of action will include both cognitive and behavioral strategies. Basically, you want to combine a positive thought or self-statement with taking action. Here is an example of an action plan that will get you through a challenging moment. When faced with an urge or craving, try this surefire recipe:

Cognitive Strategies (talking yourself through it)

◆ Smoking is not an option, so I need to find an alternative solution.

◆ This craving will go away in a few minutes, as long as I redirect my attention elsewhere.

Behavioral Strategies (taking action)

◆ Chew gum, cloves, mint toothpicks, or a straw.

◆ Go somewhere else, at least for a few minutes.

◆ Go for a walk or do some other form of physical activity.

◆ Call a friend.

◆ Brush my teeth.

◆ Recite reasons to quit.

One of the all-time greatest behavioral strategies is to take out that Jar of Kick-Butt that you've been putting your smoked cigarettes into all week. Add about one-half inch of water to the bottom of the jar and take a good look at it. One of the quickest ways to kill an urge is to open the jar and take a nice Biiig whiff. Be sure to keep this gross but highly effective tool handy for your next craving. Also, be sure to go to our Web site and download our recipe for Jar of Kick-Butt soup.

Once you've determined which strategies work the best for you in particular situations, you will be able to automatically execute the plan. At that point, you will know you are well on your way to the smoke-free life that you deserve.

Fine-Tune Your Strategic Plan

Note which strategies worked well and which ones did not. Think about where you need to add in more strategies. Get creative! Visit Web sites and chat rooms that offer ideas. Remember to try new things, and never ever pre-judge the value of a strategy until you've tried it. If you do, you will definitely miss out on some great ideas.

Think through your next 24-hour period. Actually take a mental walk through your day. (This should be done the night before whenever possible.) Picture yourself waking up, getting ready for your day, running errands, meeting people, eating meals, and so on. Picture yourself doing all of these things without smoking. Identify as many situations as possible where you might be presented with an urge to light up. Then write those situations in the following Buttkicker box.

Buttkicker

1. List the specific challenges you expect to encounter over the next 24 hours.

_____

_____

2. Write at least three strategies (Plans A, B, and C) you can use to overcome each challenge.

_____

_____

_____

Time for Goodies!

Now it's time to treat yourself to that reward you promised in yesterday's contract. Remember, these short-term rewards are well deserved and must be given as close to the time that you accomplished your goal as possible. Their value to you must be in sync with the amount of effort put forth. And remember to include nonfood rewards.

No way to pay for those nice rewards? Beginning with how many packs you purchased each month, calculate the real dollar amount that you used to spend on cigarettes.

The amount of money saved from not smoking quickly becomes mind-bogglingly significant. We suggest that you use this fund toward two types of rewards. Use about one-fourth to one-half toward your short-term goals that you give to yourself on a daily or weekly basis. Use the rest for some great long-term goals. Long-term can mean anywhere from a month to a year.

Smoking Signals

Ciggy-Piggy Bank is the storage house for all sums you've collected from the money you normally would have spent on cigarettes.

Buttkicker
Cash Stash

Dollar amount spent on tobacco-related products each month:
$_____ divided by 30 (days)
= $_____ (amount saved each day as a nonsmoker)
Add this amount to your *Ciggy-Piggy Bank* every day. (You can also add in an I.O.U. on a daily basis, converting it to real cash each week if you prefer.)

Buttkicker

Now that you've got great motivation and good momentum, it's time to put your commitment in writing again.

24 Hour Commit to Quit Contract

I promise to do whatever it takes to remain smoke-free for the next 24 hours. From now until __ o'clock on _____,
I will handle each craving a new way because I know that I'm only a puff away from a pack a day. The reward that I will give to myself for accomplishing this feat is _____

_____.

Signed: _____   Date: _____

The Least You Need to Know

◆ Recognize every cigarette that you haven't smoked in the last 24 hours.

◆ Your level of comfort may have dropped much lower than it was 24 hours ago. This is normal, and you will see it go back up over the next few days or so.

◆ Each day that you choose not to smoke brings you closer to your personal goal of a smoke-free life.

◆ Withdrawal symptoms are temporary.

◆ For the first few weeks, avoid high-risk situations that might tempt you to smoke.

◆ A strong plan of action will include both cognitive and behavioral strategies.

Chapter 7

Celebrating One Week Smoke-Free!

In This Chapter

- ◆ Review your first week of quitting and fine-tune your master plan
- ◆ Learn from challenges
- ◆ Determine your most effective strategies
- ◆ Master the top four ways to prevent relapse
- ◆ Sign your contract for week number two

Completing your first week as a nonsmoker is yet another milestone. It's a great time to assess and make any necessary changes to your master plan. Just as you've done before, you will want to hone in on the strategies that are working for you and discard the ones that aren't.

This chapter will help you master your best four ways of preventing relapses. You will learn how to practice handling your high-risk situations and sign another contract that will begin your second week as a nonsmoker. Let's get started!

Taking a Look at Your First Week of Quitting Smoking

Your quit day was a week ago, and no doubt it's been a very l-o-n-g week ago. How have you done? How are you doing now? First, let's go to the check-in station in the next exercise. After that, read the next section and choose the subheading that applies to your specific situation.

Buttkicker

Check-In Station

On a scale of 1 to 10, with a 10 being the best, most comfortable and a 1 being the worst, most miserable, how would you rate yourself at this time:

1. How comfortable are you about not smoking for the next week? ___

   1 = Extremely uncomfortable and worried. 10 = Extremely comfortable; no concerns.

2. How motivated are you to quit smoking for good? ___

   1 = Not motivated at all; I'm going to throw this book into the garbage. 10 = Extremely motivated; I'll do whatever it takes.

3. How confident are you that you will remain smoke-free for the next seven days? ___

   1 = I'm sure I won't make it. 10 = I know that I will stay quit.

4. What specific situation do you think will be your greatest challenge for the next 7 days? _____

5. What are your plans of action for this situation (Plans A, B, and C)? _____

6. How troublesome are your withdrawal symptoms, such as cravings, nervousness, difficulty concentrating, and so on? ___

   1 = Overwhelming and miserable. 10 = Completely comfortable; no discomfort.

By now, you should begin to see some changes in your scores. Below is a description of the typical changes that take place.

- **Question #1:** Your level of comfort should be getting better (or at least leveling off). If you've had a slip, however, this will not be the case for you. Also, if you can't seem to stop thinking about cigarettes, your comfort level will be bad.

- **Question #2:** Your motivation should still be high, hopefully eight or above. However, for some people, it begins to dip down a bit at this stage. If this is your experience, it's time to plan a really great reward for yourself.

- **Question #3:** Your confidence level should be holding steady; it may even be edging upward. However, it's better to be optimistically cautious and not to get overly confident. It's too early for that. Hope for the best, but plan for the worst. In other words, continue to plan ahead.

- **Questions #4 and #5:** Your greatest challenge for the next few days should be identified and you should have several plans of action to meet it.

- **Question #6:** Your withdrawal symptoms rating should be getting a bit better. You should notice that some symptoms are improving, while others may be persisting. By the end of the next week or two, you will definitely be over the hump. Just don't have a single puff because it tends to re-ignite the whole recovery process all over again. Keep telling yourself that smoking now is just not worth it. (And let's face it; one is never going to be enough, is it?)

Assessing Your Master Plan

At this point, either your master plan is working beautifully or it still needs some fine-tuning. Let's take a look at how many times your plan has helped pull you through cravings and temptations successfully.

Now take a good look at the number of cigarettes you didn't smoke this week. Each of those not-smoked cigarettes represents an individual success for you—a battle won. Isn't that incredible? Now that's progress.

You're doing it; you're regaining your control, one cigarette at a time. And that's what you need to keep doing. Continue to focus on one day at a time, or reduce it to one hour, or even one half-hour, at a time.

> **Buttkicker** _____
>
> Calculate the number of cigarettes you *didn't* smoke in the past week. Fill in the blanks based upon how much you were smoking two weeks ago:
>
> ____ cigarettes per day × 7 = ____
>
> (Subtract any cigarettes that you may have slipped with; one puff of a cigarette is the same as one full cigarette) = ____
>
> Cigarettes not smoked this week: ____ Wow!

The Bigger the Challenge, the More You Can Learn

Some people call them problems. We prefer to use the term challenges (and we recommend that you do the same). Life is full of challenges, and each one represents an opportunity to learn and grow. So, whether or not you met the challenge, there is knowledge, and therefore power, to be gained. Let's take a look at your recent challenges related to quitting smoking.

> **Buttkicker** _____
>
> What have been your biggest challenges over the past week? List at least two specific situations where you wanted a cigarette. Then describe how you handled each situation. What did you do that worked? What did you do that didn't work? How would you handle things differently next time?
>
> **1.** _____
>
> **2.** _____

If It Ain't Broke, Don't Fix It

Let's focus on what's been working for you. Which specific strategies have you been using the most? Think about the techniques that have helped you get by without the first cigarette in the morning, the one at bedtime, and the one when you're feeling stressed or angry.

Buttkicker

Make a list of your top three strategies for each category (cognitive and behavioral). These responses should become automatic, going into effect almost without your even having to think about it. We've included some examples, and if any of them are your favorites, feel free to circle them.

Cognitive Strategies

◆ I tell myself that one is never enough and that any more than that is too many.

◆ I recite my top five reasons to quit.

◆ I find the humor in the situation, laugh, and remind myself that the craving goes away in a few minutes, whether I light up or not.

1. _____
2. _____
3. _____

Behavioral Strategies

◆ Drink water with lemon   ◆ Take slow, deep breaths
◆ Go for a walk   ◆ Chew some gum
◆ Tell some jokes   ◆ Brush my teeth
◆ Draw a picture or write a letter

1. _____
2. _____
3. _____

Relapse Prevention Kit

Many smokers who quit relapse within the first two weeks. In order to make sure you're not one of them, read through the following relapse prevention kit. We've included four power-packed "Relapse Preventers" to help you win your war on tobacco.

To Heck with This!

There are two things you need to know about a relapse. Every relapse begins with a slip, with a single puff of a cigarette, and most slips begin with giving yourself permission to "fall off the wagon." This permission often takes the form of you saying to yourself, "Oh, to heck with it."

Relapse Preventer #1: Have an answer ready for the "Oh, to heck with it" comment. Some successful ex-smokers we know have used answers like "What do you mean, 'To heck with it?' I am bigger and stronger than this addiction, and I'm in control now. Smoking isn't even an option. I am choosing not to smoke because I want (list all of your most important reasons to quit here), and that's that."

Romancing the Cigarette

Many people who relapse placed themselves in high-risk situations prior to the actual relapse. For example, they start going to bars again or hanging around certain smokers. They start to watch other people smoking, wishing that they, too, could taste that tobacco flavor in their mouths again. Others begin talking about the positives of smoking instead of the negatives. This is called *"romancing the cigarette,"* and it's just like setting the stage for a relapse.

This is why using the term "slip" is slightly misleading. A slip usually isn't like suddenly slipping on a banana peel. It's more like setting up all of the props on a stage before the play begins. "Relapsers" often find themselves setting the stage and then giving themselves permission to "slip."

Relapse Preventer #2: If you find yourself romancing the cigarette, call yourself on it. Refocus your attention on the negatives of smoking and the positives of quitting. Remind yourself that you have chosen to free yourself from this deadly addiction for many good reasons and that you are in charge.

Abstinence Violation Effect

The abstinence violation effect is a phenomenon common to most types of drug addiction. Basically, if a person who has been avoiding a particular drug or behavior for a period of time has a slip-up, he or she may feel like there is no point in continuing with the avoidance.

It's extremely important that you do everything within your power to stay 100 percent tobacco-free (no puffs or anything). Doing so will make your quitting endeavor as smooth and comfortable as possible.

Relapse Preventer #3: Stop yourself before you finish that first cigarette. Without thinking about it, take yourself and all of the cigarettes in sight to the toilet bowl and flush them immediately. Don't hesitate, just do it. Make sure every last one gets in there. Next, drink a glass of cold water and take some deep, refreshing breaths. Remind yourself that you are fighting a vicious addiction, but that you are the stronger one. State your reasons for quitting out loud.

Visualizing Success

One of the best ways to gain the expertise that only comes with experience is by increasing your opportunities for practice. The best and safest way for you to do this is through visualization.

Relapse Preventer #4: First, think about your most challenging situations as a new nonsmoker. Think about all past and future situations that have and will make quitting smoking difficult for you. Then, vividly picture yourself in each situation but with the preferred outcome—not smoking. Make the scenario as real as possible by mentally focusing on details, such as who else is there, what they're wearing, or the temperature of the room. Think about what you might be able to do, say, or think that would get you through successfully, without a cigarette. Visualize yourself specifically getting through each situation and emerging as a happy nonsmoker.

Customizing Your Commit to Quit Contracts

At this point, many people choose to complete a weekly contract, while others prefer to continue to go one day at a time. You should choose the time period that is best for you, resetting it whenever necessary.

> **Buttkicker**
> **Commit to Quit Contract**
>
> I promise to do whatever it takes to remain smoke-free for the next ___ days. From now until __ o'clock on _____, I will handle each craving a new way because I know that I'm only a puff away from a pack a day. The reward that I will give to myself for accomplishing this feat is _____ _____.
>
> Signed: _____ Date: _____

The Least You Need to Know

♦ After completing your first week as a nonsmoker, assess and make any necessary changes to your master plan.

♦ If you've had a recent slip, it's a sign that you need to strengthen your commitment and coping strategies. After a slip-up, throw out all of your cigarettes and keep going forward.

♦ Many people who relapse placed themselves in high-risk situations prior to the actual relapse.

♦ Visualize yourself getting through high-risk situations.

Chapter **8**

Slips and Relapses

In This Chapter

- ◆ Getting rid of your cigarettes
- ◆ Deciding if you're ready to quit
- ◆ Why you relapsed
- ◆ Learning from your relapses
- ◆ Preventing further relapses

Slipping up goes hand in hand with quitting smoking. In fact, most people who quit smoking relapse five or six times before they finally quit for good. After a relapse, it's not uncommon to feel as though you have completely failed or that you must not be ready to quit smoking yet. Lots of people say, "The heck with it," and quit trying to stop smoking. It's important to put your relapses in perspective and see them for what they really are: opportunities to learn.

If you've ever experienced a relapse, this chapter is for you. Even if you've never had a relapse, reading this chapter is a good idea because it may help prevent one from happening in the first place. It will also prepare you for handling this situation if you are ever in it. You will read about specific strategies that help you quickly recover from a relapse and get right back up on the horse. Above all, you will learn how to turn a relapse into a stepping stone to success.

Get Rid of 'Em

The first thing you should do after a slip-up or a relapse is to remove any temptations to smoke by throwing out any and all cigarettes that are around you. Don't put them anywhere but in the garbage. You should even pour water over them; that way there is no possibility that you can pick through the garbage and smoke them. (Yes, we know all about this phenomenon.)

The next thing you should do is sit down and give yourself a good talking to. You need to decide if it's worth giving it another try. Think about all of your reasons to quit, and then ask yourself if you are really ready to stop for good. Was the slip-up just a temporary detour, or was it a sign that you really aren't ready to quit smoking yet?

How can you tell if you are ready to quit again? Start by reviewing your reasons for quitting in the first place. Are they still very important to you? Are you still motivated to quit? Is now the right time to be quitting, or are there too many stressful events going on in your life? Are you prepared to let go of your slip-up and view it as a quit-smoking tool, something that can shed some light on what you need to do differently the next time you are faced with a relapse? Are you prepared to commend yourself for trying to quit in the first place, rather than condemn yourself for smoking again?

If you have answered "no" to some of these questions, then you may need to reorganize and work on your motivation. If that's the case, then this chapter will be of great help. Or maybe you need to wait a little longer before trying to quit again. Perhaps things are just too stressful right now for you to give quitting smoking the attention it will require. If this is the case, you might be better off focusing your time and energy on resolving your stresses. That way, you will be able to give it a really good shot in the near future. After a few weeks or months, when the time is right, you can try quitting again.

If you have answered "yes" to most of these questions, then you're ready to give it another shot. Hooray for you! You can quit immediately, right on the spot, or you can set another quit date for one to two weeks from now. What you do depends upon your ability to understand why the slip happened and your confidence in your abilities to prevent another one from occurring. If your confidence level is high, finish reading this chapter and quit right away. If you feel a little shaky or unclear about what happened, set another quit date in one to two weeks, and focus your attention on figuring out why you relapsed, building up your motivation, and further solidifying your quit-smoking plan.

Playing Detective

Relapses can occur in a variety of settings and for a variety of reasons. Recognizing why a relapse has occurred is the key to figuring out what it really represents and how to prevent it from recurring. Let's take a look at some of the most common situations where relapses occur:

- Feeling isolated
- Pressures at work
- Being at a party
- Noticing weight gain
- Feeling bored
- Hanging out with unsupportive smokers

- Feeling very lonely
- Overwhelming stress
- Having an argument
- Drinking alcohol
- Feeling depressed
- Feeling anxious

Stress

One of the most common reasons for relapsing is stress. When our sensibilities are overwhelmed by stress, we tend to fall back on old ways of coping. Stress can be easy to recognize, like when you're about to go into a meeting at work and your heart is racing, or when you are stuck in traffic and stressed out because you're late for an appointment.

Stress can also be more subtle, such as when you worry about making a new car payment or moving to a new house. Subtle stress has a way of eventually wearing you down to the point where you are at risk for relapsing. You can use smoking as an escape from the stress, and it's all too easy to get used to using your cigarettes again for this reason.

How prepared are you for the stresses in your life? Are you aware of the things that stress you out? Think back to your relapse. Were you experiencing any stressors?

Buttkicker

If stress was the reason behind your relapse, you probably weren't ready for it. However, that can be fixed so that the next time you will be better prepared.

Fill in the lines that follow by writing in the stresses that were behind your relapse. Also describe how your body let you know that you were under stress. Last, fill in the specific coping strategy you're going to use the next time one of these situations arises.

My Stressors	My Road Signs	My New Strategy
Late for work	Clenched teeth	Slow, deep breaths

Loneliness and Depression

Maybe you relapsed because you got too lonely. When people get too lonely, they may get anxious and feel down. As they look for ways to rid themselves of the anxiety-provoking loneliness, it's not uncommon to think about reaching for a cigarette. The nicotine lifts you up and distracts you from your loneliness. Some people who have relapsed for this reason say the cigarette is like having a friend there with you.

If loneliness was your reason for relapsing, did you predict you might feel this way when you quit, or did it come as a surprise? Most people are surprised to find that they feel lonely after quitting because it's hard to know all of the things cigarettes were doing for you until you go without them.

But now you know, and now you can take steps to prevent loneliness from causing another relapse. Here's an exercise that can help:

Buttkicker

Look at the entire week in your life when your relapse occurred. Pick out the times of day when you felt lonely. Then, come up with some strategies that will prevent you from getting too lonely. Some ideas include going to the mall, volunteering at a hospital, calling friends or family, writing letters, or using a computer and going on to the Internet. Having a plan to immediately enact when you get lonely can help deter a relapse.

Lonely Time	Alternative Activity
_____	_____
_____	_____
_____	_____

Depression is one of the biggest culprits when it comes to relapsing. Remember, many people who smoke use the nicotine in their cigarettes to self-treat depression. You may have unmasked a depression that was already there, but your smoking just kept it under wraps all of these years. If you suspect this is the case, you should talk to your doctor about your possible depression and ways to treat it. If you weren't already using the quit-smoking pill Bupropion, it might be a good idea to discuss this option with your doctor, too. The good news about depression is that it is almost always treatable.

On the other hand, you may not have had an underlying depressive disorder, but instead your feelings of depression are a symptom of nicotine withdrawal. Such a development is very common, especially if you smoked 10 or more cigarettes a day and quit cold turkey. If depression from withdrawal was behind your relapse, consider using some form of nicotine replacement therapy. If you already are, make sure your dose is correct. For example, you may not be chewing enough of the gum. Remember, most people need to start with the highest dose of these products when they are quitting. Don't make things harder on yourself by starting with too low of a dose. Also consider getting some regular exercise, outdoors if possible. Exercise is a good mood booster.

Many people who quit and get depressed report that they feel sad because they miss smoking. In fact, it's not uncommon to feel like you have lost a good friend or to feel as though you have given up something you really enjoyed doing. If this is your case, consider whether you're really giving something up or whether the truth is that you're gaining health and freedom from an addiction instead. Think about your so-called "friend," and remind yourself that friends don't try to kill you. This is a good example of where the phrase, "With friends like these, who needs enemies?" really applies.

If feeling depressed is one reason why you relapsed, it's important to figure out exactly why you're depressed. Until you do, you won't know how to deal with those feelings. In fact, it's unfair to ask yourself to deal with quitting smoking unless you deal with your depression first.

Anger

Allowing yourself to become too angry can also lead to a relapse. It's not too hard to find all sorts of opportunities to get angry every day. Sometimes, anger just comes over you like a storm. Wanting to smoke a cigarette at these times is very common because it can physically get you out of an angry situation and it's also relaxing and calming.

If you relapsed when you were angry, try to figure out why your anger resulted in smoking. Also, decide if smoking really helped the situation. Chances are good that whatever made you angry enough to choose to smoke in the first place was still there when you finished puffing away. And to make matters worse, you probably felt horrible after you relapsed.

Think of better ways to release your anger that don't include smoking. Maybe you could have just left the room and gone outside for a few minutes, or maybe you could have tried avoiding the situations that tend to irritate you. Again, exercise is a good way to blow off steam and balance your mind. Having a good strategy for dealing with this emotion can prevent further relapses from occurring.

Buttkicker

If your quit-smoking plan doesn't include ways to deal with anger, you may be setting yourself up for another relapse. List the types of situations in which you tend to find yourself feeling angry, then list things you can do besides smoking to help blow off some steam. Include things like deep breathing, going for a walk, talking it through with a friend, and exercising.

Makes Me Angry   **Alternatives to Smoking**

_____   _____

_____   _____

_____   _____

You may need to come back to this list the next time you get angry. Also, don't be surprised if you have to practice the alternatives a few times before they automatically pop into your mind the next time you get angry. Remember, practice makes perfect.

Quitting One Step at a Time

One of the best ways to avoid a relapse is to look back at what led to the relapse and break it down into steps. Doing so will help you visualize what specific steps led to the relapse and allow you to hone in on opportunities to alter the outcome. For example, say your refrigerator breaks down. You call a repairman who says you have to buy a new one. (They always do.) Then you go to the mall and are surprised by how expensive refrigerators are. Since you don't have enough money in your checking account to pay for a new refrigerator, you have to put it on a credit card. But your credit card is close to being maxed out, and this purchase puts you at your limit. As you walk out of the store, you begin to worry about your financial situation, and you even get into a squabble with your spouse. On the way home, you stop off at the store, buy a pack of cigarettes, open them up, and smoke one. Next, you find yourself feeling very guilty, so you smoke some more.

How could this story have ended up with you remaining smoke-free? First, understand that you're not alone: Most people deal with this level of stress from time to time, and most are able to cope without resorting to nicotine. Second, once you start to feel this way, it's up to you to put your strategy of delay into action.

For example, on your way home while you were thinking about stopping off to buy cigarettes, you could have reminded yourself that the craving will go away soon, whether or not you light up. (And getting yourself addicted again would have added only one more problem to your list.) Instead of stopping off to buy some cigarettes, maybe you could have driven out of the parking lot and gone out for a strenuous walk, gotten a snack, or bought a cup of coffee.

The point is to see the craving as a signal that you're feeling overwhelmed. You need to distract yourself briefly until the craving goes away, and then you can deal with your real problem directly. Even if you got as far as buying the cigarettes, maybe you could have done something drastic like thrown them down the toilet. And just because you started to smoke one doesn't mean you couldn't have immediately stopped and tried some deep breathing or some other way to avoid smoking.

Buttkicker

Think about your last relapse and break it down into as many steps as you can. Then, try to plug in alternative steps that would have led you down a different path, one that didn't result in a relapse. If you have relapsed more than once, try to do this activity for each one. By spending the time doing this activity, you will be more aware of what leads you to a potential relapse, and you will be better able to prevent other ones from happening.

The Temptations

A wise person said that temptation is at the root of all evil. That person probably knew a few smokers because temptation is frequently at the root of many relapses. Many people find that the temptation to smoke is the greatest when they are around other people who are smoking. The following is a list of some of the most tempting times to have a cigarette:

- In a bar
- During a work break
- With friends who smoke
- At a party
- With a spouse who smokes
- Living with someone who smokes

Temptation may have been at the root of your relapse. Where were you when the relapse occurred? Who were you hanging out with? Were you out with your smoking friends without a plan for turning down any cigarettes that they offered you?

Maybe you need to avoid certain social settings, such as bars or smoke-filled coffeehouses, for a while, or at least until you are absolutely certain of your resolve not to smoke. If you live with someone who smokes, ask that he or she smoke in another room or outside when you're home. Let your friends know that you're trying to quit, and ask that they not offer you any cigarettes. Think about turning the people who may tempt you into supporters by asking for their help. Who knows, a few may even want to quit right along with you.

Perhaps the most common reason for starting to smoke again is fear of weight gain. No matter how well they're doing without the nicotine, some people would rather smoke than put on any weight at all. Unfortunately, weight gain after quitting is all too common. However, just because you have gained 5 pounds doesn't automatically mean that you are on your way to gaining 20—or even that a little weight gain isn't worth the incredible health benefits you gain from not smoking.

If you've gained weight, take a closer look at your daily habits before you put all the blame on quitting. Since you quit, how many days a week have you exercised? If it's one or two, try four to five. Increasing your amount and intensity of exercise is a great way to burn calories and keep the weight gain down to a minimum.

> **Quit Tips** _____
> Use an NRT to keep your weight gain to a minimum. If you're not using a nicotine replacement product, consider doing so because these medications can help keep the weight off long enough for you to develop better eating patterns and get used to exercising regularly.

Since you quit, what has happened to your eating patterns? Have you substituted food for smoking? Are you having a lot of cravings for sweets? Keep a record of the foods you are eating. Are they high in fat? Consider eating healthier snacks or lessening your portion sizes.

The Least You Need to Know

◆ After a slip-up, throw away your cigarettes.

◆ Decide if you are ready to quit again, and if life is too stressful now, put off quitting for a while.

◆ Have a plan to deal with stressful situations.

◆ Relapsing is a normal and expected part of quitting.

◆ Use your relapse as a stepping stone to success.

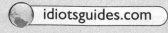

Contents at a Glance